MW01318967

To Bob,

May God's grace & mercy lead & guide you daily.

Sincerely,

Vielia

Request for permission to make copies of any part of this work should be mailed to:
Permissions Department, Witty Writings Publishing, 9065 Alsandair Court, Reno, NV 89506

Printed in the United States of America

In the beginning was the Word, and the Word was with God, and the Word was God.
St. John 1:1(KJV)

That if thou shall confess with thy mouth the Lord Jesus and shall believe in thine heart that God has raised him from the dead thou shall be saved.
Romans 10:9

Acknowledgment

I want to thank God for using me to write this devotional and I am honored to be one of His born again children. I would like to thank my family, mom and son Joshua for demonstrating God's unconditional love. I would like to thank my Church family, Solomon's Temple, under the leadership of Bishop James & Linda Holloway who's Bible based teachings and guidance cultivate personal relationships with God the Father, Son and Holy Spirit. Lastly I want to thank God for each of you as you grow in your walk with the Lord.

Vielia

Preface Opening

I expect God! I am expecting God to do greater things than He has ever done before and to keep every one of His promises. Lord keep the vision ever before me that I may reach for it with both hands. "Write the vision that they may run who read it, though the vision may tarry, wait for it, it shall surely come and not lie."

January 1

Declaration:

The Lord's perfect and divine will for my life is the goal. To live to please God in all I do is my mission. To surrender my own will is the way. My purpose is to share the love of Christ with the world, through my actions. That is my lifestyle, not mere words and rituals. I will give God the Glory, Honor, and Praise. That is why I am created. He created me, I didn't create Him! May I obey this declaration all the days of the year.

January 2

In realizing who God is, we come to understand our frailty and utmost dependence on Him. The more we depend and rely on God, the more we get to know Him and the power of His might. Earthly knowledge can be enlightening, but down the road it will lead to a burdensome reality of our true state (without God I can do nothing). But thanks be to God who is our hope of Glory and Jesus Christ our Savior. Therefore we can say "I can do all things through Christ who strengthens me."

January 3

My goal is to wait on God to bring about His perfect divine will for my life. While I am waiting, I will "wait" or serve the Lord in all that I do. Praise and worship, giving, obedience, helping others, fasting, and praying are all essential to a spiritual walk with God. God is waiting on us to carry out these daily acts of service, while we are waiting on Him to fulfill his promises. What type of service are you rendering to the Lord as you "wait" on Him?

January 4

Intimacy with Jesus Christ is the ultimate of all encounters ever experienced on earth. Once a person has achieved an intimate relationship with Christ, nothing else will ever satisfy to this degree. It is the epitome of all things experienced on earth. I pray that we all come to enjoy an intimate relationship with Christ with the time we are given here on earth.

January 5

When you fast, pray, and consecrate yourself before the Lord, allow Him to kill your flesh that you may experience new levels of worship. During this time, your relationship with God should grow stronger. Your desire should be to go behind the veil and into the most holy of holies where the Lord God resides. You may need to repent for reducing your prayer time down to a dogmatic timed chore that benefits no one. Through fasting and praying, we become intimate with our Lord God.

January 6

"I can do all things through Christ which strengthens me." The key in the Christian walk for being able to do "all things" is through **Christ**. *In our own ability, we can do nothing. It is in God that we live, move, and have our being. If we are mindful of this, there is no room for pride or to get puffed up in our own fleshly abilities and accomplishments. Remember that God is always in control. Trust and believe in Him, because God never fails.*

January 7

Have you ever come to a point on this Christian journey were you are unsure of what to do next? Trust and believe God with your all and try not to murmur, complain, or have any doubts. Things that you don't understand or necessarily agree with God about still require you to be faithful. Continue to pray earnestly and fervently, and through it all, learn who God is and how awesome He is. If God told you His plans you wouldn't understand it anyway, so trust Him, His credit is good.

January 8

God's Word says that eyes haven't seen, ears haven't heard, neither has it entered the heart of man the good things that God has prepared for those who love Him. We can't even imagine the wonderful plans God has in store for His children. God also says that He is able to do exceedingly, abundantly, above all that we ask or think, according to the power that works in us. So fasten your seatbelt, fellow spaceship companions, because the blessings of God that He has ordained for us are out of this world.

January 9

We must present our bodies as a living sacrifice, holy and acceptable unto God which is our reasonable service or the least that we could do. Doing this will glorify God in our bodies and it will magnify our spirits with His Spirit. When sacrificing our bodies, we are not fulfilling the lusts of the flesh through what we want, think or feel, but instead, what God desires. It is as if we are being burned alive, purifying our bodies, hearts, souls, and minds.

January 10

Salvation is the gift from God for all of mankind, but we must receive and accept the gift, it is never forced upon us. I thank God for receiving the wonderful gift of salvation in my life. It is our calling as Christians, to share the good news of Jesus and the Cross so that others may also have the opportunity to receive this precious gift. Let's not be selfish and keep this gift all to ourselves; let a dying world know the love of God awaits them. Who have you shared the Good News with lately?

January 11

My desire is to obey God and not grieve the Holy Spirit. If we truly want peace and joy in this Christian walk, obedience to God is very essential. We'll still have trials, but we can endure trials and tribulations knowing that we have obeyed God, and won't have to suffer needlessly because of disobedience. We obey God because it is the right thing to do, not to get a reward or payoff from Him. Our rewards may not all come in this life, but when we see His face in heaven it will not be worthy to compare with our present day sufferings.

January 12

During our alone times with God is when He shows us our true selves. It is hurtful when we get a glimpse of what we are really like. Sometimes we have no idea we are as far off the mark concerning the standards of God in certain areas of our lives. God can only show us ourselves a little at a time because we couldn't handle seeing too much all at once; It would crush our spirits. God saves us all at once, but he delivers us day by day. Thank God for the alone times with Him, it is during these times that the old man can pass away to behold the new.

January 13

When we know the plagues (diseases) of our own heart, we can truly see how God's grace has kept us, in spite of ourselves. We can only know the plagues of our heart as we go before God in true prayer and quiet time. When this occurs, then God can begin to reveal things to us. We can't let the enemy use the distractions of our daily lives to keep us from truly hearing from God. In our prayer time, God's voice, and His alone, must prevail.

January 14

At some point on this Christian journey we have all said, and should say "Lord hear I am, send me." But when we don't like the assignment given to us, we don't go. What is needed for the Lord to send us is a total denial of our own will and motives, and a total commitment to God's will, and His way. Neither can we question God, it is a journey void of our input of how things should be done. When this happens, then God can send us!

January 15

I love the Lord and I thank Him for the resurrection of my new life in Him. The old things have passed away, and now all things have become new. The will of God is our sanctification. Sanctification is not a dress code (no make-up or jewelry, long dresses, etc.), it is a heart transplant. We have the heart of God to honor Him in all our ways. When we are sanctified, we are set apart for the Master's use. God wants to use us to minister to a dying world. Those who have died to the flesh (sanctification), can minister to the spiritual dead to revive them.

January 16

If you strongly desire to know the call of God upon your life (your ministry field in the body of Christ), be assured that He will reveal it to you. God reveals it through prayer, study time in His word, other people and fellowship with Him. Then it is totally up to you to accept the call on your life. Surrendering to the call of God gives peace even during the storm. Understand that what God calls you to do may not be what you would have picked of your own free will.

January 17

To be in a relationship with God where you understand His call on your life, then do everything out of sheer love for Him is the goal for a beautiful amazing spiritual walk with God. Get excited about having such a level of spiritual growth whereby you attain this level of intimacy with the living God on a daily basis. Your constant prayer should be; not my will, but Gods will be done in me, through me and for me. Give up your fleshly rights and put on the righteousness of Christ.

January 18

Loyalty is a rare thing these days. It is hard to find a loyal friend, spouse, or worker. If we learn how to be loyal in our spiritual relationship to God the Father and His son Jesus Christ (obeying the Word of God), then we will know how to be loyal in our earthly, carnal relationships with one another. God is totally loyal to us (faithful), for He has said He will never leave us nor forsake us. I pray we return the loyalty, and not leave or turn away from Him.

January 19

If I have learned anything from my trials, it is that God is REAL and He is good all the time. I have come to know and experience God like never before as I go through the trials He has designed for me. As you face your next trial, endure your current trial, or catch a breath from your last trial, always remember that God is real and longs to reveal Himself to you. Always remember that no matter what circumstance we may find ourselves in, God is real and worthy to be praised, reverenced and given the glory.

January 20

There is nothing continuously dependable in this world, but God. Therefore, to depend on anything else is useless. In God we live, move and have our being. God is our breath of life, no breath, no life. Our lives are dependent upon the ability to breathe, so we must depend on God to supply us with His breath of Life. The Bible tells us that God breathed the breath of life into man, and man became a living soul. Are you a living soul or the walking dead? Life in Christ makes the difference.

January 21

I always want to be so in love with God that my heart skips a beat when I think and meditate on Him and how good He is. I get so excited about being alone in His presence and experiencing His divine revelations. We should always enter His gates with Thanksgiving and His courts with Praise, where we can find rest, peace, healing, joy, and comfort in the time of need. Let's be so in love with God that we take no thought for our own will but only for the will of God.

January 22

One of the slogans I incorporate into my Christian walk is "Look unto God". We must remember to look to God for direction, counsel, salvation, healing, deliverance, understanding, patience, love, peace, kindness, strength, prosperity, and any and everything that pertains to life. Trust that God is all we need Him to be, in every area of our lives, and more. Call on Him, look to Him and He will be there waiting for you. "I will lift up my eyes to the hills, from whence comes my help; my help comes from the Lord."

January 23

The word of God says: "be ye transformed by the renewing of your minds." And again it says: "let this mind be in you that was also in Christ Jesus." Once our minds are renewed in Christ, then we can begin to think like Him. Once we begin to think like Christ then we will begin to act or imitate Christ. When we imitate Christ we are glorifying Him to the world. Live out your Christian journey in such a manner that unbelievers and sinners will say: "what must I do to be saved?"

January 24

Prayer Break:

"God, my greatest desire is to have my whole life mastered by You. Please God, plant me in Your perfect will so that I may be of service to You all the days of my life. I whole heartedly want to live to please You. I pray God that this year You will have Your way in every single area of my life. I want nothing left not uncovered by You. Lord search me through and through and if You find anything at all that shouldn't be, please take it out, purge me, and strengthen me. In Jesus' holy name, Amen."

January 25

I am expecting breakthroughs, healings, miracles, and deliverance, for the children of God this year. I expect God to do exceedingly abundantly above all that I ask or even can think, according to the power (Holy Spirit) that works in me. I expect God to show up in our lives and leave His supernatural marks of answered prayers. I thank God for equipping us to lead others to His saving grace, love, power, and mercy. I know that we can do all things through Christ who strengthens us. Amen.

January 26

"Lord I want to be consecrated for Your use."
To be consecrated means to be set aside for God's divine use. As Christians, we need to "come out from among them and be separate." Consecration is a lifestyle that must be cultivated daily. Ask the Holy Spirit to have its way in your life, to consecrate you more and more each day. If we are not being a vessel of honor used by the Lord, then that only leaves one other option, a vessel of dishonor being used by the devil. There is no middle ground, so determine today to yield completely to God.

January 27

Lord, teach me to rest solely in You and to not let anxieties deter me from cultivating my relationship with You. Lord, teach me to give everything over to You and leave it all with You. I in my own strength and knowledge cannot do anything about the situations that I come up against. Until You move on my behalf or give me divine revelation knowledge, nothing will change. If I say I trust You, then I must trust You, even when it hurts, I don't understand, or I don't agree.

January 28

Lord God and Jesus Christ, please have mercy upon me. Forgive me for being obstinate, selfish, rebellious, disobedient, and (______________). My only desire is to please you. Lord God I thank You for another chance to repent of all my sins, both known and unknown that I have committed. I want to get things right before You according to Your Word. Lord, I give You all the glory and honor that is due Your name. Hallelujah! Jesus is alive and worthy to be praised. Amen.

January 29

Sometimes we try to put our relationship with God in a box. Meaning that we reduce Him to something we try to control or predict, instead of letting God control and guide us through faith. We try to figure God out, what He will do next and how He will do it. That type of logical thinking and deductive reasoning will never work in an authentic relationship with God. God must be in complete control at all times and we must trust Him at all times. We never know when or how God will move so we have to be ready at all times.

January 30

Can you keep a secret? Most of us can't keep information (good, bad or neutral), all to ourselves without telling at least one other person, it is just human nature. Sometimes God reveals thing to us, speaks to our hearts or may give us a dream or vision and instructs us to tell no one or ask anyone their thoughts or opinions. "Lord please teach me to not share or ask of others what you have given me privately." When we consult the flesh, we give the devil the opportunity to give his thoughts and opinions as well.

January 31

Salvation only happens when God allows it, that is, when He calls us out of darkness into His marvelous light. "With love and kindness have I drawn them." As Christians, God chose us, we didn't choose Him; we only accepted His invitation. It's just like when a bride and groom send out wedding invitations to potential guest. None of us has any control over whether or not we are invited to the ceremony, but once invited, we must decide whether or not we will accept the invitation. Have you accepted Christ's invitation?

For I know the thoughts that I think toward you, says the Lord, thoughts of peace, and not of evil, to give you an expected end. Jeremiah 29:11

February 1

As Christians, why do we focus so much on our burdens and so little on the Burden Bearer? "Lord God, help us to get the focus off of ourselves and put it on You." When we magnify God and not our problems, then and only then can God's will be done on earth as it is in heaven. What is this will? It is to Preach the Gospel to the ends of the earth. "Lord, teach us and grant us wisdom, knowledge, and understanding as You anoint us to spread the Gospel of Jesus Christ to a dying world."

February 2

Each time Jesus performed a miracle by feeding large masses of people with little food, He blessed it first, then He broke it. I've heard it said that God uses brokenness in our lives to accomplish His will. A key point in being broken and then used by God, is that He first blesses. So if you are in a broken situation, state of mind, or have a broken heart, know that the Lord is very near to you. Above all, know and understand that you are blessed by God who is about to provide a miracle just for you because He loves you very much.

February 3

"I press toward the mark for the prize of the high calling of God in Christ Jesus." Have you noticed that sometimes (many times), during this Christian journey, you have to really press your way through? I don't know why, but I used to think that once I accepted Christ as Lord of my life, that He would deliver me from tests and trials as soon as I prayed and asked Him (in Jesus' name of course). But it doesn't work that way. We are made (like Christ) in the trial, not in the deliverance. So we must press forward, even if it's only by an inch some days.

February 4

"…These are those who come out of the great tribulation…" As John describes these saints, who can't be numbered, worshiping before the throne in Heaven, it is clear that making it to Heaven will not be a leisurely stroll in the park. Joining a congregation, serving on a committee, being a volunteer, attending services three times a week, and tithing isn't all that our Christian journey is about. It is about staying the course and trusting that God is who He says He is and will do what He says He will do, when everything in you wants to quit.

February 5

If you know of anyone looking for a Savior, share God's resume (the Holy Bible), with them. He's the artists that created the heavens and earth and all their beauty. He's the architect that created Noah's Ark and Solomon's Temple. He's the Chef who prepared meals to feed thousands of men, women, and children. He's the healer who gave sight to the blind, mobility to the lame, healing to sick, and life to the dead. He is the Father who gave His only begotten Son to die for our sins so we may be reconciled or reunited back to Him.

February 6

Sometimes as Christians, we act as if we are doing God a favor. We don't have to go to church; we get to go to church. We don't have to pray; we get to pray. We don't have to serve God; we get to serve God. We don't have to sing psalms and have praise and worship; we get to sing psalms, praise and worship God. Serving God should never be seen as a chore or something to check off of our "to do" list. God is to be first in our life at all times and at all costs. Remember, God doesn't need us, in order to exist, we need God in order to exist.

February 7

Lord God, teach us to get a hold of You in our prayer time. Let us not be self seeking just for answers, but to whole heartedly seek You out of love and for fellowship. In getting a hold of You in prayer, we can rest in Your presence and in Your Word. Then, in Your own timing the answers to our prayers will come and we will be able to handle how You may answer. Lord please forgive us for treating You like a Santa Clause who dispenses gifts off a list of requests. Lord help us to seek Your Kingdom first, and then all other things will be added to us.

February 8

Salvation is free (it is the gift of God), but it will cost you. We must be Holy (untainted by evil, pure) as God is. Most of us are not prepared for the cost of sanctification. It will cost us everything that is not of God. To be set apart or sanctified means we must look and act like God the Father and Jesus Christ. If God performed a D.N.A. test, the results would come back 99.9% negative for most. Godly acts, dress codes, and scripture quoting are not sanctification. Daily consistent prayer, reading and obeying the Bible are what sanctifies and sets us apart.

February 9

Prayer Break:
"Lord please forgive me for all of my sins. I repent of getting easily wearied and troubled concerning (________). I now know that this is one of the reasons that You have saved and sanctified me. Lord help me to daily draw my strength and joy from You, as those whom You have placed in my path, may draw from me. Lord I thank You for the brokenness that will feed others in and around my life. Let the light of Christ shine in me as a testimony to Your greatness and awesome power to heal, deliver, set free and restore." Amen

February 10

"... bringing into captivity every thought that exalts itself against the knowledge of Christ." "If we keep our minds stayed on Jesus, He will keep us in perfect peace." "Be you transformed by the renewing of your mind." The mind is where the battle is fought, not in the flesh. When the enemy brings negative thoughts into our minds, we must quickly cast them out and transform them to line up with the Word of God. The Word of God shows us how to fight the good fight of faith so that we may win the battle every time.

February 11

The Christian Testimony: We are children of the most High God and we must serve Him with all of our hearts, mind, body and soul. Our souls ache and long for true fellowship with the Lord. We desire to be lead and used of God all the days of our lives. The Lord God is our all and all, and there is none like Him in all the earth above, in, or below. We love Him because He first loved us. We are more than conquerors, through Him that loved us. The sun shall not strike us by day or the moon by night. The Lord shall preserve our souls forever more.

February 12

Lord help us to hear Your voice when you speak to us. Speak Lord that we may listen, know and trust You. May we obey Your Word and commands as You lead and direct our paths. Lord, it will not always be an easy or enjoyable task to blindly trust the voice of God, but it is and will always be well worth it. Jesus said "if any man hears my voice harden not your heart." Therefore, when we hear the voice of God we must be quick to obey it, otherwise our hearts will become hardened or deaf to the voice of God. Lord forbid!

February 13

"Lord God, my earnest desire on this Christian journey is that You remove all things and people in my life that hinder me from hearing from You. I no longer want to have misplaced devotion to things, people, or projects (jobs, cars, homes, serving at church, volunteering, dress codes, giving, family, friends, or leadership). All these are blessings from God and have their rightful place in our Christian walk, but none should ever replace time spent seeking the face of God. Lord, teach me to cultivate my devotion to You that I may hear Your voice at all times.

February 14

The greatest love story ever written, told or displayed is the love the Holy Bible describes that God has for us, the sons and daughters of man. God is Love, literally. To know God is to know love. Love is an action word, not a mere emotion. Love created man in its image. Love established a covenant between God and man. Love promised, Love delivers, Love gives, Love was born of a virgin, Love died for my sins and yours. Love has Resurrection Power over heaven and earth, and hell below.

February 15

As Christians (Christ like), we must know and understand that we are walking, breathing, living testimonies of the salvation of Jesus Christ. We are to live the gospel and preach it to the uttermost ends of the earth, not just our neighbor sitting next to us on the church pew. This command is given to us directly from Jesus Christ Himself before ascending back up to heaven. At judgment time we will have to give an account for our roles in leading others to Christ or away from Christ.

February 16

We are over comers by the mere fact that we did not sub come, cave in, give up, throw in the towel, or quit to the trials or tribulations that came our way. We are still alive, serving God and giving Him the Glory because the trial didn't kill us, it made us stronger. Our faith was on trial and won. The devil meant it for evil, but God meant it for our good. Share your testimony of how God helped you overcome a particular trial, it will inspire others who may be going through a difficult time to trust and believe God for their victory.

February 17

The Lord knows how much we can bear. His yoke is easy and his burden is light. We must remember these words when the enemy uses our circumstances to attack our minds with the spirit of depression. We must cast our cares upon the Lord because He cares for us. The Word of God says "Come unto Me all you who labor and are heavy burdened, and I will give you rest for your weary souls." And "I will give you the garment of praise for the spirit of heaviness." So when we get tired in our mind, body and spirit, give it over to God, Who will give us peaceful rest.

February 18

Never get stagnant or comfortable in your walk with God. We must arise and go on to the next level in Christ. The past must sleep in the bosom of Christ. Sometimes this may be a very difficult thing to accept and do, (bury the past). Never the less, not our will, but God's will be done in our lives. With strength from God along with faith and the Holy Spirit as our comforter, we must go out into the irresistible future with Jesus Christ. He will "do exceedingly, abundantly above all that we ask or can even think."

February 19

"This is the day that the Lord has made, I will rejoice and be glad in it." Determine in your mind to rejoice in this day. Resolve to get up and get going, even if you are not all that inspired to get up or get going. Only through the grace of God can we persevere through the drudgeries that sometimes accompany our daily lives. When we persevere we will find grace to help in our time of need. Arise, shine, and give God the glory. Let us thank God for transforming the drudgery into the expectancy. Your expectation will not be cut off.

February 20

"...I must be about my Father's business." If we take care of Gods business, He will take care of ours. Gods business for us is to share the Gospel with the world and give Him all the Praise, Honor, and Glory. The Bible tells us in Mathew 6:25-32, not to worry about our lives or daily provisions, because God has it all under His control. God is Jehovah Jireh our provider. The thoughts and plans God has for us are more abundant than anything we could ever imagine for ourselves. So "seek first the kingdom of God and all other things will be added to you."

February 21

Prayer Break:
"Lord God teach us to abandon (totally sell out) ourselves to You so that You may get the best out of us. Teach us to love beyond ourselves. Redirect our thoughts and cleanse us from all unrighteousness. We thank You Lord that although at times we may not be of any use to You (because of sinful deeds), we are always of value to You. Lord we thank You because as Your children You always love us unconditionally, in spite of our words and deeds. Help us to learn to display this Agape type of love in our Christian walk." Amen.

February 22

I pray that every born again, spirit filled Christian embraces tenacity (persistent in maintaining or adhering to; not easily pulled apart.) Being tenacious is a vital character trait for all Christians and essential in our walk of faith. Jesus Christ will win and all of us who have fought the good fight of faith, endured until the end, and stayed the course, will reign with Him. "To him that overcomes, I will grant to sit with Me on my throne, as I also overcame and sat down with my Father on His throne."

February 23

When something is no longer growing, then it is dead. The more I learn, grow, and mature in Christ, the harder the battles that come upon me. That is the price of war and we are in a war. I believe we sometimes forget how gruesome war can be on its soldiers. The more we grow and mature in the Lord, the more we die to the flesh. The more we die to the flesh, the more battles we fight between the spirit and the flesh. God's Word says the spirit is in opposition of the flesh, and vice versa. But don't fret this battle is not ours, it's the Lords, and He has already won.

February 24

We say that we are sold out for Jesus and His concerns are our concerns, that His will shall be done in our lives, and that we want God to get all the glory. But most often, we find ourselves repenting of "the small foxes that spoil the vine." Maybe we didn't handle the situation at work, home, or in traffic in a way that honors God. Perhaps in a particular situation we misrepresented God and lost the opportunity to win a soul over to Christ. And for that Lord God we are most sorrowful, please forgive.

February 25

Lord teach us to destitute ourselves so that we may lead our family members, co-workers, friends, neighbors, strangers, and even our enemies to Christ. To do this it will take the love of God ruling our hearts, mind, body and soul. This type of love doesn't have to be returned from men but drives us to go on in Jesus Christ. All souls are Gods and as His servants we are not to show partiality, have respect of persons or only care about those who care about us. Non Christians do that. Christians are called to a higher standard of love.

February 26

It is nearly impossible to believe in what we don't or can't understand. When we face trials or situations that we cannot comprehend, we begin to doubt if God is able, just because we are not able. But Gods abilities are not and will never be based upon our abilities or comprehension levels. If we could always figure God out, predict when and how He will move in a situation, then we have put ourselves in the place of God. Lord forgive us for reducing Your sovereignty down to only working when we can see it or know how it will work.

February 27

Declaration:

I look to the Lord Jesus Christ to do those things, which in the natural realm, seem almost impossible. God specializes in the impossible and He can do what no other power can do! I believe with all my heart that God Almighty is the one and only true and living God. In God is the fullness of the God head (Father, Son, and Holy Spirit.) All His promises are yes and amen. There is no failure in God. God is not a man that He should lie, nor the son of man that He should repent, if He said it, it will come to pass. I believe God!

February 28

Lord God, help me not to make my own common sense decisions, and then ask You to bless them. I desire to rely on the resurrected life of Jesus Christ down to the very core of my being. I bring my will, mind, body, soul, and emotions under the power of the Holy Spirit. I want Christ magnified in my life. Let me not get bound up in rituals or legalities of service to You, but to always pursue an intimate relationship with You first and foremost.

February 29

When the business of life starts to close in on you, remember Jesus' example to steal away and pray. Learn to cultivate a prayer life that is consistent and intimate. Notice I didn't say how long it needs to be, because that is between you and God. But I will tell you this, the more time you spend with God, the more time you will want to spend with God. Our prayer life needs to be consistent because the Word of God says we are to pray without ceasing, and to pray in season and out of season. Our prayers need to be intimate (personal) and real with God.

The blessing of the Lord, it maketh rich, and He adds no sorrow with it
Proverbs 10:22

March 1

The Word of God is the standard by which we are to live. It can be used as a mirror to show us how we line up with the Word of God. As we read the Bible, Gods standards are revealed to us. As we examine our lives based upon the Word of God, the reflection of ourselves we see in that mirror can hurt. Until God reveals to us how far off the mark we are, we are oblivious to our true reflection. But the love of God, which covers a multitude of sins, only shows us how we line up with His Word, bit by bit, so that we don't become utterly dismayed.

March 2

Why did you decide to make Jesus your Lord and Savior? Was it for fire protection from hell? Was it because you want to please someone in your life or get them to stop nagging you about going to church? Was it because all of your family members say they are Christians and you didn't want to be the only one who wasn't? Was it because you had come to the end of yourself, no longer thought you had it all together or knew all the answers and deep inside knew that with all you have been through, only God could have kept you this long? God loves you, no matter why!

March 3

When the love of God dwells in us, we will manifest this love by our actions. There are no conditions with God's love, it is not based upon if we do or don't do this, or if we will or won't go there. When we begin to love unconditionally as God loves us, then we will unconsciously and automatically be our brother's keeper. We will be so in tuned with the Holy Spirit that we will not doubt or question the prompting He gives us to help someone, give to someone or just befriend someone. We will freely go about our Fathers business.

March 4

Do you know what ministry gift God has equipped you with for His Kingdom work? Do you know what the Word of God says the gifts are? Do you know how the gifts are utilized for the Kingdom of God? If your answer to these questions is yes, then great! Are you using them or are they lying dormant? If the answer to any of these questions is no, then turn to the Word of God for guidance. Pray and read the book of Acts chapter twelve and the book of Romans chapter twelve. Seek the face of God and allow Him to reveal your call to ministry.

March 5

Ministry Calling Prayer:

Lord God, please reveal to me the ministry calling that You have placed upon my life. Lord I understand that before the foundations of the world You knew me, predestined me, sanctified me and called me to do Kingdom work. Lord God, have Your way in my life and cause me to be intimately in touch with You, that I may know the call You placed upon my life. Lord God help me to discern and fulfill what I am created and regenerated to do in my Christian journey. I thank You for Your divine revelation. Amen

March 6

Christians must keep the work done on the Cross in sight. We must be able to keep the eyes of our spirit open to the risen Christ, especially when our natural vision gets blurred from tests and trials. We have to always remember that this is a blind faith walk with God, and we are unable to predict which way the path leads, turns, or stops. But we should always thank God that He is ever present with us, even when we feel like we are all alone. God is faithful and promises in His Word that He will never leave us nor forsake us.

March 7

Do you have a best friend? What makes that person a best friend? Well understand this, "No greater love has any man than this, that a Man would lay down His life for a friend." That friend who died for each of us is Jesus! He is the epitome of what a best friend represents. Jesus is the type of friend who will never let you down. You can fellowship with Him through the Word of God and prayer. He is anxiously waiting to be the Friend your heart and soul needs. Go on and try Jesus, you can trust Him with all your cares.

March 8

Prayer Break

It's me again Lord, standing in the need of prayer. Lord I pray for deliverance from (____). I am beginning to realize that this requires letting go of everything and everyone and solely relying on You. I need You Lord to lead me and guide me every step of the way, in every area of my life, each and every day. It is no longer what I want to accomplish, but what God wants to accomplish through me. I want to be a willing participant in the plan of God for my life. I thank You Lord for hearing and answering my prayers. In Jesus' name, Amen.

March 9

As we live out each day, growing closer and more intimate with God, it becomes apparent that we don't know the detailed plans that He has for us. We know the thoughts He thinks towards us are of peace, not of evil and He has promised to give us a future and a hope, but there is no book we can look at to give us the play by play. Each day, and night, we must seek God for direction and clarity with the major, life changing decisions we face. The Word of God has promised that when we acknowledge the Lord in all our ways, He will direct our paths.

March 10

The Word of God says that "obedience is better than sacrifice." But more often than not, obedience ***is*** *a sacrifice! When I am facing a battle and my flesh wants to be gratified through one of the senses, but the word of God says to mortify (kill) the flesh with its passions and desires, then I must sacrifice my wants and desires and obey God. Obeying God isn't always easy, fun, nor do I always agree or understand it. But, our Heavenly Father loves us and He knows what's best for us and we can always trust Him.*

March 11

What are the visions and dreams God has revealed to you? Do they seem farfetched at this point in your life? Can you see how God is going to bring them to pass? Remember, this is not a sight walk, but a faith walk with God. The dreams and visions that God reveals, write them down, so that when they come to pass, everyone will know it was God and not you. "Write the vision plainly so they may run who read it, though it tarries, wait, for it shall surely come and not lie." God's "super" plus your natural produces a miracle every time.

March 12

Praise Break:

Hallelujah! Thank You Jesus and I love You. Glory to God. I will give myself over to total abandonment to my God. Let me not be found giving only to receive something in return. Lord my desire is to be a sell out to You and for You. Although I am not fully aware of everything total abandonment may entail, I do know that You, Lord God, equip those whom You have called. Holy Spirit, have Your way in my life, this day and every day. Amen.

March 13

"For the joy that was set before Him He endured the cross." What a powerful scripture of God's love. Have you ever wanted to know the joy that was before Him? Reconciliation, restored fellowship, and the biggest family reunion ever! God sowed His Son, to reap a family. Jesus was able to endure the cross because of the joy the Father, Son, and Holy Spirit would have in reclaiming us back from the enemy. Child birth is similar in that a woman must endure the pain, suffering, and sometimes death, of labor for the joy of having a child.

March 14

Prayer Break:

"Lord God I yield (totally surrender or give over) to You my mind, body and soul. It is a struggle for me because some habits I really enjoy, and would not give up if I didn't have too. To some people, these habits may seem harmless or not that bad. However, if I desire them, or it, more than the Word of God, prayer, fasting or fellowship with God, then I must yield it all over to Him. Holy Spirit, please give me the strength to yield my entire life over to You." Amen.

March 15

I used to try to figure out how and when God would move in my life. I tried to predict Gods every move (as if I were the one in control.) Unfortunately for me, I had the Omnipresent (present at all times everywhere) and Omnipotent (all powerful) God in my own little box. Needless to say, my whole God philosophy exploded in my face and I was left in total dismay and utter confusion. God is the Creator of all things, and will never be dictated to by His creation.

March 16

"Walk in the light as He is in the light and you will not fulfill the lusts of the flesh." If we are mindful of the judgment seat of Christ, then perhaps we will continually walk in Gods light, giving no space to the enemy to distract or lead us over to darkness. Gods light is equal or synonymous to His presence. Therefore, if we stay in His light, then we will stay in His presence. When the light comes in, darkness must flee.

March 17

Love Letter:

Lord God, I love You and want more of You. My Father, which art in heaven, I thank You for always being there for me. You have never let me down, Ever! I want my Daddy to pick me up into His loving arms, and give me the biggest and longest hug I have ever known. I feel safe in the arms of my Father. He protects and loves me, in spite of me. Thank You Lord for adopting me into Your heavenly family.

Love Always, Your child,

(______________).

March 18

Daily purge me Lord God that I may be kept clean in my walk with You. I desire perfect holiness in my life, to the point that neither I, nor anyone else who comes in contact with me sees or hears me, but Jesus Christ and His Word manifested. As I press toward the mark for the prize, help me to remember that to be like Jesus is my goal. To do the will of my Father who sent me is my purpose. I declare that God is first and foremost in my life, Always!

March 19

I now understand why I have no idea on a day to day, hour to hour, minute to minute basis what to expect next or what God will do next in my life. It is because a life of faith never fully knows the path that it is traveling; only that God is in control leading and guiding every step of the way. Our testimony of Gods faithfulness is in the not giving up or out, and persevering to the end. Remember that the just shall live by faith, simply put, we must apply faith to every situation, at all times. For we walk by faith, not by sight.

March 20

We must continue to ask, seek, and knock, that we may get to know God better and get a perfect understanding of who God is. We ***are*** *God's will. What a revelation that statements allows. It is a joy to know that being alive in God is His will for each of us and that He will instruct us every day on how to fulfill His purposes. We must wholly submit to the Lord that we may be one as Jesus and God were one! In His final hours on earth, Jesus prayed to God on our behalf, "...that they may be one as We are one."*

March 21

"Faith comes by hearing, and hearing by the Word of God…God has given each man a measure of faith… Now faith is the substance of things hoped for, the evidence of things not seen…without faith it is impossible to please God…fight the good fight of faith." WOW! Faith is a lifeline between us and the kingdom of God. In this Christian journey, I pray that we keep the vessel of faith clear of blockage, strong and healthy, to prevent cardiac arrest.

March 22

Sometimes we as Christians can behave like preschoolers when we find ourselves or get caught in trouble. Christians want to blame the devil or sin for every problem. There are times when the devil does play a role, but often times so do we. When we allow unrepentant sin to come in and run rampant, we can't give the devil credit for that. We must be more aware of our own natural ability to let sins go unchecked. "For all have sinned and come short of the Glory of God."

March 23

Prayer Break:

"Lord God, I am sorry for known and unknown sins that I have committed. If there is anything in me that shouldn't be, please take it out and strengthen me. I want to stand before You spotless, blameless and with a repented and grateful heart. Purge me with hyssop; cleanse me from all unrighteousness and filthiness of the flesh. Lord help me to know the plagues of my own heart that I may pray earnestly and effectively. In Jesus' name I pray, Amen."

March 24

Lord please help us to decrease in our carnal desires, actions and thinking, so that Your presence may increase in our lives. As You increase and permeate every area of our being, use us to influence those we come in contact with to desire a Christ centered life. Give us the mind to surrender and humble ourselves under the mighty hand of God. Let the joy of the Lord be our strength and salvation. Lord, You are more than able to keep us; my prayer is that we will always want to be kept by You.

March 25

Prayer Break:

"Lord God, we need Your deliverance daily. Forgive us our sins. Help us to always be God chasers and not people, status or material things chasers. Lord help us to faithfully run the race that is before us, enduring to the very end so we may obtain an imperishable crown. Your Word says You will never leave us, nor forsake us. Bind the enemy and all his imps (Satan's fallen angelic helpers) and cast them into the horrible pit of hell. Thank you for giving us power over the enemy. In Jesus' name Amen!"

March 26

"Blessed are the pure in heart; for they shall see God…whatsoever things are pure; meditate on them…but the wisdom that is from above is first pure…pure and undefiled religion before God and the Father is to visit orphans and widows and to keep yourself unspotted from the world." Purity is a necessity in the kingdom of God. To accomplish His will and to come before His presence, we must repent, and then proceed in communion with the pure Holy God. Thank the Lord; we have that right of fellowship through Jesus Christ.

March 27

Going higher in God is always achieved through tribulations, tests and trials. It is never a promotion based upon the number of years served, your title, position or status. Going higher in God also doesn't mean that in the natural realm (what the world or public can see), you will simultaneously be elevated. The reason why is because when God elevates our character, our outside circumstances don't always immediately change. It is always an inner change that occurs first. God works from the inside out in our lives.

March 28

The Lord has given everyone a measure of faith, which means that all of our faith levels are not equal. There are, unfortunately, some who have no faith, in God (that is). Some have little faith, some have great faith, and others have the gift of faith. The Lord can increase our faith in Him (through tests and trials) and impart faith (reveal His presence and power) unto those who don't believe. But know that without faith, it is impossible to please God.

March 29

"…And those who are still alive will be caught up to meet Him in the sky." This scripture describes the rapture of God. Help us dear Lord to live rapture ready that we may be able to go back with You when You come. Forgive us for being caught up in religious doctrines, traditions, and battles that are of no necessity, nor productivity to the kingdom of God. Teach us to live, and breathe the unadulterated Word of God. Make us to be spiritually clean and pure towards You, ourselves and everyone we come in contact with.

March 30

"Pray without ceasing…watch and pray, lest you enter into temptation." It's easy for us to be hypocrites toward one another, when we are operating out of our flesh and not God's Spirit. When we are lead by the Holy Spirit we can genuinely discern (know) how to pray and intercede for one another. Lord God please deliver us from the spirit of hypocrisy and impart unto us the spirit of intercessory prayer. Jesus intercedes on our behalf to the Lord God, and as His followers, we are to do the same. The salvation of all souls is priceless.

March 31

I love to worship the Lord because I can forget about my surroundings and be close to God and God can be close to me. When I worship God, my spirit is filled with joy, love, peace, happiness, and excitement. It is something I can never experience, no matter the circumstance, outside of worshiping God. We were created to be in continuous worship and fellowship with God. I find it hard to understand how those who do not worship God while on earth will want to spend eternity in continuous praise and worship unto the Lord!

Now unto him that is able to do exceeding abundantly above all that we ask or think, according to the power that worketh in us
Ephesians 3:20

April 1

Sometimes we get so caught up in the cares of this world that we become heartless and desensitize the mind, heart and will of God. Continuous intercessory prayer, a lifestyle of fasting, plus praise and worship will help to keep us from being stale in our relationship with God. If our walk with God is fresh, then we will have a sensitive and discerning spirit. When we come into contact with others and they are suffering in an area of their life, we are to bear their burdens as if they were our own. The strong must bear the infirmities of the weak.

April 2

I pray that we all might receive our sight of the Lord Jesus Christ. Sometimes I think we look right at Jesus and don't recognize Him because we are spiritually blinded of the things of God. We must have spiritual insight into the mind and workings of God if we are to be His followers. We must recognize the voice, the hand, and the moving of the One we say we believe in, in order for Him to lead us and not be deceived by another.

April 3

If we truly learn from our past mistakes, repent and turn from them, then they should no longer have any power over us. If and when we encounter our past, there should be no fear. Our testimony should be to the glory of God, for turning the darkness into day. "What the devil meant for bad, God meant for our good. The Lord knows how much we can bear, and He will never put more on us than we can bear. For we know that all things (good and bad) work together for the good of them who love the Lord and are called according to His purpose."

April 4

We are made in the fire (trials and tribulations), and then brought forth as vessels of honor, sanctified and useful for the Master, and ready for every good work. Until we go through our very own tailor made trials and are tried in the furnace of affliction, we only have pseudo (unreal) faith. Faith that has never been through anything isn't faith at all. Real faith is what is left standing after everything else has been demolished in the fiery trial.

April 5

Prayer Break:

"Thank You Lord Jesus for the price You paid for me at Calvary that I might be reconciled back to a right relationship with God my Father. The Son of Man was in agony for my soul and died in my place. I am truly grateful that Jesus gave His life for mine and I surrender mine to Him whole heartedly. Lord open up the eyes of those who do not know You or have a personal relationship with You so that they may fully understand the work You did for them on the Cross. In the precious name of Jesus, Amen."

April 6

Oh the cross, what a wonderful saving device. Without it, no one can be reconciled to God, but with it, everyone has the victory in Christ Jesus. The Word of God says that Jesus never murmured or complained while on the cross, but many Christians murmur and complain when bearing their cross. We have to stay focused and not let the devil distract nor steal our joy. Christ endured the cross for the joy that was set before Him, and we can bear the cross because weeping may endure for a night, but joy always comes in the morning.

April 7

The closer we grow in our relationship with Christ, the more He reveals our current state of being. When He does this, it is heart wrenching for us to see ourselves. We think we have it all together for the most part, until God shines His light on the situation. When this occurs, we must repent and ask God to help us get to the character of His Son Jesus, which is the true identity we want shining through at us and the world.

April 8

Jesus died for us that we might live for Him. We have to take Jesus' work on the cross personal. When Jesus said, "Father forgive them for they know not what they do", insert your name in the slot that says them, and own your role in His death. When something is personal we value it more. As Christians, we must have more value toward the work on the Cross so that we may have more value for the life we live in Jesus.

April 9

Paul saw Jesus on his way to Damascus and it changed Paul's life forever. Once we have a true and genuine Jesus encounter, our lives will never be the same. It is then that our Christian walk really begins its journey. We have a clearer picture of what the Master wants from His servants. We no longer are religious or ritualistic, but we become spiritual and compassionate for the things of God.

April 10

Prayer Break:

"Lord search me through and through; and if You find anything in me that should not be, I ask that You take it out and strengthen me. My desire is to be whole in You. Lord please kill all traces of sin that may dwell in me. Let only the Spirit of Christ reign in my mortal body. I don't want to hold on to any form or stench of sin. I repent and desire to be released from sin and ask that You have Your way in my life. In Jesus' name, Amen."

April 11

Our desire as Christians should be for the Holy Spirit to invade and take over our lives and bodies. Our hearts need to be pleasing to God and obedient to all of His commands. There is in us, no power to accomplish Gods will without the manifestation of the Holy Spirit. God must be the One to orchestrate our lives.

April 12

Lord God, please help me to continually let go of everything not of Your divine will for my life, even if my grip is tight. Help me to let go of everything that is not like You or has any traces of sin. Lord don't let me give up and please don't get weary of me. I will continue to press toward the mark for the prize of the high calling of God in Christ Jesus.

April 13

Most people have a difficult time giving their burdens over to the Lord and leaving them with Him. We may start off with the intent of allowing God to carry our burdens, but when things don't happen when, where, and how we believe they ought to happen, we take our burdens back from God. We try to handle them ourselves, and only make things harder or even sometimes worse. Just leave it all in His hands, because He can and will handle it in His own timing.

April 14

Do you love God more than, food, clothes, cars, your job, your spouse, your kids, your body . . . or whatever else it is that keeps you from totally surrendering to Him. What is it that you have placed more value, honor, love, or devotion to other than God Almighty? Sometimes we have to dig deep to discover what we idolize, in place of God. Ask God to search your heart and mind for anything that might be worshiped by you other than God. When he reveals it, repent and move on.

April 15

Lord reveal to me the areas that I have been failing You by being disobedient and not keeping my vows that I have made to You. If I have made promises to You in any area, and have slacked on them or totally abandoned them, please forgive me. Please Lord, tear down the "high places" that linger and hinder my spiritual walk with You. With the help of the Holy Spirit, I will pay my vows to You because You are a worthy and faithful God. Thank You for this opportunity to begin again and make good on my vows.

April 16

I think that we as Christians sometimes live as if Jesus isn't coming back soon and we have time to do all that God has assigned us to do. The Bible tells us that we need to be about our Fathers business while it is day, because when the night comes, no man can work. So while we are alive, we must do what God has called us to do, because if we die, and haven't completed our assignments, then night has come and we can no longer work. On the day of judgment, we want to hear our Master say "Well done My good and faithful servant."

April 17

One of the reasons we sometimes believe we are defeated on this Christian journey is because we let our emotions rule and not the Word of God. We try to handle spiritual issues through our fleshly emotions; I want, I think, I feel. These are not the weapons of our warfare. Our weapons are mighty through God and are able to pull down every stronghold that we will ever encounter. Some of the weapons we have include prayer, worship, fasting, and the Word of God. Today, let's determine in our minds to prepare for spiritual battle!

April 18

Lord Jesus, get us ready for Your surprise visits. These are the visits that reveal who we are and what is in us. They are like pop quizzes in life to see if we have been studying and are prepared. We love You Lord God and are so grateful that You visit us, whether it be by surprise or invitation. When we invite God we expect Him to show up, and show out. When He drops in on us, He expects us to be prepared. Always remember that the God we serve is always on time and waiting to bless us with every heavenly blessing.

April 19

Sometimes we are prepared or on the lookout for the big crises, test, or trial, but not the small ones that creep in unaware. Lord keep us alert of the least things and aware of the undercurrents. After making it through the trials and being back in the will and peace of God, we never want to go astray again. Although we cannot forecast where or when the next temptation will come (and they will surely come), we know that being kept by God's power is our only safety net.

April 20

Do you believe that God is more than able to fulfill His promises that He has given you? Well He is! Not only is He able, but He is also willing to fulfill them. It is Gods desire to bless us with the promises from His Word, prayer, preaching, teaching and anointed prophets. We need to remember that with each of Gods promises that He makes to His children, there are requirements and conditions we must follow in order to inherit them. We can't live a life of sin and expect the promises of God to prevail in our lives.

April 21

"Praise Break"

Oh Lord, how excellent is thy name, in all the earth! Every knee shall bow and every tongue confess that thou art Lord. Our God is an awesome God, He reigns from heaven above with wisdom, power and love. The Lord God is Jehovah Jireh, my provider. I will bow down and worship Hïm for this is the day that the Lord has made, I shall rejoice and be glad in it. Oh what a friend we have in Jesus. We worship You Lord, we magnify Your name, and we give You the Glory and the honor too. Oh how I love Jesus, because He first loved me."

April 22

Have you ever had someone to fail you are let you down? We all have. Sometimes we even fail ourselves or let ourselves down. In this human body, we are destined to fail or disappoint at some point in our lives. Despite our every attempt to follow through on our promises or have someone depend on us, we fall short. But thanks be to God that He has never failed us. God never fails! Love never fails. God is love, therefore God, who is love, never fails! Aren't you glad that we can trust that God will always be there for us and never let us down.

April 23

Whether a person believes in Jesus Christ or not, we all must face God for ourselves and take responsibility for how we have responded to His work on the Cross. Knowing this, we cannot allow anything or anyone to hinder this face off. We must live in a manner that is continuously pleasing to God, and to please Him we must believe that Jesus is His Son and died and rose again for our sins. When we are face to face with God, I pray each of us will hear "Well done, My good and faithful servant, enter now into My rest."

April 24

A devoted life to God, must begin with a spiritual awaking. Once awake, you must cultivate your relationship with the Lord. This is a lifelong process. We are to continue to grow and mature in the knowledge of God that He may impart unto us the wisdom and understanding we need to experience Him in all of His glory. The Bible tells us that in all we get, be sure to get an understanding. Just when we think we know and understand God, He reveals a new level of His awesome presence and power.

April 25

The sign of an obedient child toward their parent is when they do their best whether they feel like it or not. So we must go on and perform the tasks God has given us to do whether we feel at our best or at our worst. In the end, it is not our emotions that are to rule and guide us, but the Word of God. Most days, many of us don't feel like going to work, but we know that we must in order to eat and pay bills. The same is true with God, His kingdom work must be done.

April 26

"Choose you this day whom you will serve." Choices become habits, habits become character and character is who we really are. God take our character and make it over to be in the image of Jesus Christ. Take away all traditions and self imposed convictions that misrepresent the Lord God. Make us to be so in tuned and sensitive to the Holy Spirit that we are able to change courses whenever God leads and not to think it is a trick of the enemy.

April 27

Lord God, when I ask for deliverance, healing, a job, a mate, a house, a car, a financial breakthrough or to be debt free, I am not asking for these things in the place of having a real relationship with You. Nothing can take the place of God in my life and what He means to me. I am asking that I may know You and Your awesome power even more, and then tell of Your goodness, even the more.

April 28

Thank You Lord Jesus! I believe that I am finally approaching the point of total abandonment to You. The point where I say "God I don't know what You are going to do in my life or how You will do it, but I am not worried about it because I trust You. Lord I feel free in You, as if a heavy weight and burden has been lifted from me. Thank You for allowing me to cast all my burdens upon You and for caring for me.

April 29

Dear Lord God, I don't know how, when, or where You are going to move in my finances, physical health, emotional health, mental health, or spiritual walk with You; but I know, that I know, that I know, that You will give me a great future and an expectant end. This present day is a gift from God, my past is covered by the blood of Jesus and tomorrow is held in Your precious hands. Being in the presence of God today, assures me that He will certainly show up and show out, without a doubt.

April 30

"For God so loved the world that He gave…" God is love. Apart from God we cannot experience the true nature of love. Outside of God, our view and understanding of love is selfishly warped. We must first be in God for Him to teach us to love ourselves, one another and God Himself. It is an absolute pleasure to love God and one another once we learn from Him what love truly is. It is an action, unselfish and deliberately expressed, and motivated to please its object of affection. That is Love.

May 1

Live by faith. Live by faith. Live by faith. This message is repeated over and over again in the Word of God. Why is this message one of the major points in the Bible? I'll tell you why, because it is essential to having a relationship with God. It is often repeated because we have a tendency to wander off from living by faith. Instead we begin living by sight (using near sighted vision at best) or by tangible things (things we can feel or touch). I pray that God will help us on a daily basis to live and walk with Him by faith.

May 2

As a doer of the Word and not a hearer only, what active role do you have in your local church body? Do you sing in the choir or praise team, play an instrument, teach ministry classes, praise dance, serve on the hospitality committee, witness committee, meals on wheels committee, work in the children's ministry or the clean up committee? Each and every believer joined to a local church has to be more than a bench warmer. This is an active game that needs every player on the field. Choose a position to play and be committed.

May 3

The work of an intercessor (to plead or mediate on another's behalf), requires dying out to our own selfish thoughts and concerns and tapping into the will of God for a particular person and/or situation. We must trust that God is sovereign and His way is always right. What the enemy means for bad, God will always use for our good. Each of us has to live (stay, abide, reside) on the battlefield of prayer, in season (peaceful times) and out of season (troubled times). "Pray without ceasing."

May 4

"…And the Spirit Himself makes intercession for us with groanings which cannot be uttered." The need for intercessory prayer is tremendous. Lord if there are any hindrances in our lives that negate us interceding, please remove them and strengthen us in You. Oh Lord, let us wholly identify with You and Your interests so that we may declare the blood of Jesus against the enemy. "For greater is He who is in Me, than he who is in the world." In the end we win. The Saints of God win with Jesus on our side!

May 5

God's plan of salvation was in place from the beginning of time. God had always planned to reconcile (re-establish friendship between) us back to Him through the precious blood of His Son, Jesus Christ. Therefore we must view salvation as the precious gift that it truly is. This gift has been waiting for each of us to open since the day of our natural birth. Let us take time now to thank our heavenly Father for His awesome gift of salvation. If you haven't done so already, open up yours today, or share the gift with an unbeliever.

May 6

Patience is a virtue. "Let patience posses your souls." Thank You Lord for being patient and gentle with us, and evolving us into the revelation of Jesus Christ. Help us Lord God to show patience and gentleness when around others. Lord please mature each of us in the area of patience. We must remember that we are all striving on a daily basis to be more like Jesus. None of us are perfect. Thank You Lord for not giving up on us and help us not to give up on one another as well, because the Bible declares that we are our brothers' keeper.

May 7

There are only two types of people that God recognizes. The saved and the unsaved! You have either confessed Jesus as your Savior or you have not, it is just that simple. Whether you call yourself a Baptist, Catholic, Evangelical, Lutheran, Protestant, Pentecostal, Jew, Muslim, Hindu or Atheist, God recognizes the work of Jesus on the Cross only. It is just like clothing, there are only two things that can cover your waist area; pants or skirts. All else is just a variation of one of the two. Whether the pants are long, short, wool or plaid, they are still pants.

May 8

"...On this rock I will build My church and the gates of Hell will not prevail against it." If the Lord builds the house who then can tear it down? "And no one can lay another foundation, but which has already been laid, which is Jesus of Nazareth." If God is the architect and Master Builder then how great and solid will the house be? We have to build our solid foundation on the Word of God. Determine in your heart that no matter how beautiful the finished project, God and God alone will get all the Glory.

May 9

Thank You Lord Jesus for stretching me and aiming me toward Your purpose for my life. Although at times I have not always been pliable to the stretching and have sometimes gone astray, I thank You for Your faithfulness. God, You always know what is best for me You will only give me Your best. I will be patient during the process but help me not to murmur or complain. I may not like the process or understand all of it, but I trust God!

May 10

Take the initiative, stop hesitating, and make the first step. "Faith without works is dead, being alone." We must add virtue (power) to our faith. Add Godly action to our faith life. We have to **do** something. Stop talking, wishing, complaining and dreaming. We must make our visions the reality God has called them to be. God will not do what He has given us the power to do. God has done His part, now we must do ours.

May 11

Love is only possible and edifying, that is encouraging, in its most pure state. If we have the love of God within us, then we are able to love as He has called us to, unselfishly. We cannot give to others nor display in our actions and attitudes, what we do not posses. Only God can teach us to suffer long with love because that is His way with us. Without the love of God, then we are drawing from an empty well. Jesus is the well of life.

May 12

"Are any sick among you, call for the elders and let them pray…The prayer of faith will save the sick, and the Lord will raise them up, if they have committed sins they shall be forgiven" Lord God there is healing in Your wings, and by Your stripes we are already healed. I am asking for the healing of (______). Lord raise them up from their bed of affliction that they may be a living, walking testimony to Your healing power, Amen.

May 13

"Without a vision the people will perish." Your conscience is your inner vision. We have to keep our conscience toward God and sensitive to the Holy Spirit. This will keep our paths clear and void of clutter. Be in tuned and obedient to the small still voice of the Lord and grieve not the Holy Spirit, that all may be well with our souls.

May 14

Help us Holy Spirit not to live on memories of how God has moved for us in the past. Help us to continue on in the Lord and allow the Word of God to always be alive and active in us. God desires for us to continue on in Him because there is much kingdom work to be done. The Bible is clear that "the harvest is plenty but the laborers are few."

May 15

Everything that we will ever need to accomplish the will of God in our lives, He has already given us. We must cultivate it so it can manifest in our lives to complete His purposes for each of us. We are already complete and whole in Christ, but sometimes fail to display this character in our spiritual lives. God requires us to perform the assignments He has given us and equipped us to do.

May 16

"My father is rich in houses and land…" God owns everything and being the Good Father that He is, desires to give His obedient children the desires of their hearts. He always gives us what we need, not according to our obedience, but according to His goodness. And God longs to give us the things we want, that are in His will. However, we are not to treat our relationship with God as if He is Santa Claus, spilling out wish lists to Him. The goal should be to have a genuine loving relationship with Him.

May 17

Prayer Break:
Lord Jesus, thank You for dying on the Cross, then rising from the dead with all power over the earth and hell, just to save our souls. Jesus, I pray that this earth would come to know and accept Your free gift of salvation then continue on to live in true holiness (for without holiness, no one shall see God.) Keep and strengthen the Saints of God that we may be anointed witnesses of You everywhere we are.
Amen.

May 18

Praise Break:
Lord God, thank You for this glorious opportunity to worship You and to be able to bask in Your marvelous light. God You are our source and a continuous well for us to draw from. Our goal is to please You and to be used by You. To give You praise is our purpose in life, for which we were created. You need nothing from mankind, except pure, unadulterated, perpetual praise and heartfelt devotion.

May 19

Did you know that God loves us and only wants the best for us? God also wants us to give Him our best. He wants our best in prayer, worship, giving, serving, and everything that we do. Sometimes our imperfections can be crutches not to give our best to God. However, our short comings are no surprise to God, and are no excuse for not doing our best. We must remember to do all our work as unto the Lord, not man.

May 20

Prayer Break:

Lord God, I pray for each and every family who has lost a loved one or loved ones. Please strengthen them in the Word of God and through prayer. Lord touch and heal their hearts and minds. Give back their strength in their bodies that they may go on in You and tell the world that God is good all the time and He comforts hearts. "Weeping may endure for a night, but joy comes in the morning." Amen

May 21

To seek God first and His righteousness is to actively involve God in every area of life, then perform what His Word and Spirit directs us to do. In the beginning of our Christian walk it will seem as if most of the time Gods way is contrary to what we would instinctively do. However, the closer we become to God, the less contrary His will and His way will be for us. "All these things added" will be more than our hearts and minds could ever fathom. What a blessing!

May 22

Absolute oneness with God the Father and God the Son, in our finite mortal minds may be hard to imagine. It is a perpetual state of solely existing in God, and for God. I'm sure, as disciples of Christ, we all, at some point, should have experienced this communion before. However, the goal is to live in oneness with God and Jesus, not just experience it from time to time. We should long for the time when we will live and walk in total oneness with Them.

May 23

Most of us think of infidelity (unfaithful) as it relates to married couples, family ties, friendships, or contractual agreements. But we can also be an infidel in our spiritual lives as well. Whenever we are not totally committed to God, due to outside distractions or commitments, we have been an infidel. Lord God please forgive us of our infidelities and keep us faithful, true and whole heartedly committed to You.

May 24

As Christians we have to hate sin, not the sinner, but the sin that has them bound. Lord, I hate the enemy (Satan) and all of his tactics, such as; fear, pride depression, rebellion, lust, violence and abuse. I bind up Satan and all of his fallen angels and demonic spirits and cast them into the pit of hell from whence they come. I loose the gifts of the Spirit (Galatians 5:22), to operate in the earth. "For whatever you bind on earth will be bound in heaven and whatever is loosed on earth will be loosed in Heaven." Amen.

May 25

Determine in your mind and heart that you will choose Gods best. Choosing Gods best means refusing what we consider "as good as it gets." God is the best, and only desires to give His children the best. After coming to know God and understanding His ways, you begin to notice that good just isn't good enough. It is the equivalent of mediocrity, and there is nothing mediocre about God or His children. Let us strive to destroy the mentality of mediocrity and adopt the mind set of superiority.

May 26

I expect God! I expect God to answer my prayer because I know that He hears the prayers of the righteous. I desire to have a breathing prayer life, where it is continuously natural and necessary to sustain life. God is the breath of life and I desire to be in communion with Him on each and every breath. Let me not breath only for thirty to sixty minutes a day for a specific time then be finished praying. NO, let me breathe and pray, twenty four hours a day seven days a week and not faint.

May 27

Lord God, thank You for the Holy Spirit and its power. It is the Holy Spirit of God, sent back to earth by Jesus, which dwells in the believer. When the Holy Spirit abides with us and in us, it causes us to change and become like Christ. With the power of the Holy Spirit, we are able to go and do the will of our Father, who is in heaven, without failing.

May 28

Are you actively seeking the purpose of and will of God for those whom are lost or confused? Many of us Christians are not. We simply do church, like you would do the dishes or the laundry, as if it is a chore we want over quickly so we can get to have our fun. As a Christian, we were bought at a price, our life is not our own. Let's use our life as a light.

May 29

"What so ever you ask My Father in My Name, He will give it to you." Sometimes we limit the power of God that wants to operate in our lives because we don't understand the "what so ever". It is any and everything that we can imagine and even things we can't imagine, according to the will of God. If we have faith, and are obedient to God's Word, we can ask for what so ever, and expect to receive it.

May 30

Do you ever feel as if God is answering everybody else's prayer requests, except yours? Do you ever feel like God has given everyone you know, gifts and talents that you wish you had? Well guess what? You are not alone; we all have felt this way at some point in our Christian journey. That way of thinking is a trick of the enemy to get your focus off of how God is continuously blessing you! Satan is a liar, so rebuke him quickly, and then literally count your blessings. I bet you can't even count that high!

May 31

How much does our public fame mask our private pain? Probably more than we care to admit. In front of people at work, church, and even at home, we portray someone who usually has it all together no matter what. This is a great attribute to display to the world as a faithful and trusting child of God. But at what cost is it effecting your private time with the Lord. We have to give God all our cares, disappointments, frustrations and concerns so that He can deliver and set us free. Then we can face another day with the joy of the Lord as our strength.

Brethren, I count not myself to have apprehended: but this one thing I do, forgetting those things which are behind, and reaching forth unto those things which are before
Philippians 3:13

June 1

Have you ever paid attention to the fact that God doesn't have grandchildren? He only has children. Each of us must have our very own personal relationship with the heavenly Father. If your parents and grandparents are all true worshipers of God, and pray and intercede to Him on your behalf, it isn't enough. You have to personally invite Jesus to be the Lord and Savior of your life to become a child of God. Natural children have rights and privileges, as well as an intimacy with their parents that is unmatched by any other. And so it is with God.

June 2

Have you ever noticed, that once a parent, always a parent, no matter the age of the child? No matter how old we get in the natural, we will never be older than our parents, and for most, never as wise as they are. The life experiences they have lived and shared with us protect and shield us from many mistakes and dangers. They know and can see what we can't because they have been where we are going. The same is true with our heavenly Father. He knows our beginning from the end, and only wants to protect us from dangers seen and unseen.

June 3

I must admit, sometimes I try to help God out. When I don't see how the way will be made or if I feel as if my back is up against the wall, I try to make my own miracle occur. The Word of God tells us to "stand still and see the salvation of the Lord." But how many times do we refuse to stand still and trust Him? I'm sure it's more times than we can count. God's way is always better than ours and won't stress us out in the process. Remember that "the blessing of the Lord makes us rich and adds no sorrow with it."

June 4

Praise Break:

Lord God thank You for Your grace, mercy and love everlasting. Lord, You have been so faithful to us, even when we have not been faithful to You. Thank You for allowing us another chance to repent, get delivered and set free from the yokes and bondages of sin. You are worthy to be praised and to be the center of our lives, all the days of our lives. God, You are good to us all the time, despite our many flaws and imperfections. Thank You for looking beyond our faults and seeing and addressing our needs. Amen.

June 5

What do you do when you want to leave a job, bad marriage, volunteer position, or church home, but God says Stay? You stay! God knows exactly what He is doing in your life, and you must trust Him. God has a way of turning that bad marriage into a great one, using you mightily on that job, bringing you before great people as you volunteer, and ministering to you like never before in your current church home. If God decides to release you from a situation that you feel you need to leave, He will, but in His timing and in His way.

June 6

The Bible tells us "...work out your own salvation..." The key word that most of us miss in this scripture is WORK. After accepting Christ as your Lord and Savior, salvation has occurred. However, you have to work at obeying God's Word and living in true holiness. Don't get confused, you don't work to be saved, You work to have your character be identical to Jesus' character. The Holy Spirit will not do what we can do for ourselves. We can't lie, steal, cheat, murder, etc. and believe we will get by because of salvation. It doesn't work that way.

June 7

Prayer Break:

Lord God, I pray that You are dominating every interest in my life. I am fully aware that You, oh Lord, are concerned about souls, and it is not Your will that any man, woman, boy, or girl should die in their sins and trespasses. You have given the world, Your Son Jesus to die for our sins, and for that I say Thank You. So make me to be concerned about souls that I may pray, witness, and be a light in a lost and dark world. In Jesus' name, Amen.

June 8

"Create in me a clean heart, oh Lord and renew a right spirit within me." Clean and new, doesn't it sound refreshing? Well it is! When we come to Christ we are a new creature, old things (sinful things we used to do before salvation) have passed away (under the blood of Jesus) and all things have become new. We no longer have the desire to willfully sin anymore. What a wonderful feeling to be clean and new!

June 9

"…For everyone that asks receives…" I whole heartedly believe that we have not because we ask not! God tells us to ask, seek, and knock. As a Christian, these are key principles we are to live by. In the natural, I have no problem asking for what I want, and I am even more confident in my asking with my heavenly Father. If my natural parents desire to give me the things I ask (things that aren't harmful of course), how much more will God the Father give to His children when we ask, seek, and knock, according to His divine will for each of us.

June 10

When asking our heavenly Father for the desires of our heart, we must be very careful to ask according to God's will. In order to ask according to His will, we have to know God personally and what His Word says His will is for us. This will require us to pray, study, fast, and seek God so He can reveal His divine will for each of us. Asking in His will, prevents us from asking "amiss" (out of order). So to ask God, we must seek God, and when we seek Him with all our heart, we shall find Him.

June 11

My real desires, what are they? They are God given urges that only He can fulfill. God will fulfill and meet everyone of my God given desires as I come to Him with a pure heart. God delights in giving His children the dreams and visions of their heart. As God's children, though, we must delight ourselves in Him, not for what He can give us, but for Who He is to us.

June 12

As we come to Christ, our inward man is changing (mind, emotions, and will) bit by bit. Never all at once, that only happens in the rapture. God chooses to deliver us and reveal our sinful nature to us, bit by bit. He transforms our character one issue at a time. If He showed us ourselves all at once, how bad off we really are, we could not handle it. Thank God for His deliverance.

June 13

Lord God, thank You for allowing me to be a Holy experiment as I yield solely to You. Your experiments always succeed, and never fail. They reveal to us, what You already knew about us. I count it all joy and I know that my experimental phases are working for my good. The alternative to a holy experiment would be an unholy experiment, which involves yielding to the devil. Those who yield to an unholy experiment will never get the victory or succeed in their efforts, in the long run without God.

June 14

Living and walking by faith means we are determined to abide in Jesus wherever He places us. When we are up or down, in or out, tossed and turned, it matters not what or how we feel. What matters is that we continuously abide in Jesus. This abiding is a great witness of the power of God to the unbeliever and encouragement to the body of Christ. We have to know that as Christians, we have no other choice but to abide in Jesus at all times and through every circumstance.

June 15

Character (who we are even when no one is around), what does ours say about us? Are we concerned about our character as it relates to being a child of God and representing Him? As a Christian, our character should say to the natural world; there is a better way in Jesus! The world should desire to be like us, (that is the Jesus they see displayed in our lives); we shouldn't desire to be like them. Our goal should be forming and maintaining Christ like character as taught in the Word of God.

June 16

No doubt, at times in our Christian journey, it seems it would be easier to quit or give up, than to stay in the fight. At times it is a struggle to be loyal to God in this earthly body. But don't let those thoughts stay around, cast them down. "This is the victory that has overcome the world, even our faith." We must keep our faith in God strong and when it gets weak, let God, build us back up in faith so we may continue on our way. Remember, cheer up, Jesus has overcome the world and we are more than conquerors.

June 17

If it had not been for God's grace which has kept me, where would I be? In other words, I could be the one homeless, addicted, alone, hungry, lost in sin or (_______). Lord forgive me for judging. If it had not been for God, not allowing me to be in the same situation that I judged someone else, then it would be me ***doing*** *what I judged. Lord God, please forgive each of us for judging our neighbor, enemy, or whoever. We have no space to judge, You alone God are the only Judge.*

June 18

"For with what judgment you judge, you will be judged, and with the measure you use, it will be measured back to you." My life is a personal testament of this law of judging someone and then being judged by the same measure. I didn't know that the things I judged and criticized others with in my heart would someday be my trial. But God knew, He knows what's in each of us and He will always bring about the right test to manifest what is really in us so that He can deliver us and set us free.

June 19

When we have an intimate and right relationship with God, we know how to recognize His voice. No matter what situation we may come up against, or find ourselves in, always obey His voice. We must hold on and hold out for what God has told us. Never doubt God. We are to never let the enemy place doubt or fear in our hearts. Let us never doubt in the dark times what God has told and revealed to us while in His Marvelous Light!

June 20

I find that so many of us, as Christians, are devoted to causes and creeds, but not to the will of God, nor to His Son Jesus. I believe that this is the reason so many church goers will perform church duties (ushering, singing, serving on youth ministry) without having any conviction to living holy as God is holy. Lord God, please forgive us and bring us to a devoted and holy lifestyle that focuses on being in Gods will and exemplifying Christ's character.

June 21

Lord God, forgive us for asking You to save us, over and over again. It has already been done and is a finished work. We need to use that breath in asking God to save those who have never given their lives to Christ, or may be in a back slidden condition (walked away from God). We need to pray for the salvation of our unsaved family members, friends, co-workers and strangers whom God sends across our paths. Lord teach us to selflessly pray for others that they may come to know You, even as we do.

June 22

Prayer Break:

Lord God, help me now to launch out into the priestly work of prayer, not the selfish prayers of spoiled brats, but soul saving prayers. I must get my mind off of me and what I want, think or feel, and have the mind of Christ. Your Word tells us to pray in the Spirit with groaning which cannot be uttered. When praying in the Spirit, our minds are not on ourselves, but the things of God. Amen.

June 23

I have determined and made up in my mind that sin will be what dies in my life. Many people (sadly, in the church), believe that both sin and God can co-exist in their lives. This is a lie from the pit of hell! God is holy and cannot even look upon sin, never the less live with it. Sin is from the devil. The bible is clear in telling us that "no man can serve two masters, he will love one and hate the other. We must choose this day whom we will serve; God or the devil. As for me and my house, we will serve the Lord"

June 24

Sin is the direct violation or breaking of Gods law as defined in the Holy Bible. In this day and age, some (in the church) compromise when it comes to sinful acts. Not God, He still calls it sin. If someone in the church has a talent or gift (singing, preaching, teaching, etc.), but is bound up by sins of fornication, adultery, homosexuality, lying, gossiping, stealing, etc., the church may overlook it, not deal with the issues, and promote the gifts and talents. This is sin on parade and it kills the person who sins along with the ministry that condones it.

June 25

God's Word clearly tells us that Christians are made in the fire. In other words, our spiritual lives are born and maintained through our fiery trials. Our lives can be compared to silver and gold. These natural elements must go through the fire before being used by the consumers. So it is with Christians, all of the impurities must be burned out of us to be of use to God and to those He sends our way.

June 26

Grace is Gods unmerited favor. It is nothing that we deserve or can earn; it is just graciously bestowed upon us by our loving, heavenly Father. Each of us needs God's grace on a daily basis, for without it, we would be lost. God's grace is sufficient for us, or adequate. God's overflowing favor and grace upon our lives, regardless of the situation is sufficient or enough to see us through.

June 27

The Lord God is more than able to keep that which has been committed (our lives), into His hands. God is more than qualified to handle the issues that come up in our lives. "For with God, nothing will be impossible." In this scripture verse, the words "will be" tell us that nothing in our present or our future is impossible for God. Who wouldn't trust a God who has already made a way today, and tomorrow?

June 28

"Not that I have attained, or am already perfected, but I press on that I may lay hold of that for which Christ Jesus has also laid hold of me." While in our flawed states, God chose us. We have not apprehended (taken into custody) God, but God has apprehended us, and for that we should be ecstatic. We are in the firm hold of God and no one or nothing can loose the hold that He has on us.

June 29

Christians make up the body of Christ. We are individuals with different callings, gifts and assignments. Our spiritual walks with God are personal and unique of one another. For example, it isn't a sin for women to wear pants. However, if God has personally told certain women they are not to wear pants, for His own reasons, then those particular women shouldn't wear pants. But, those same women can't criticize or judge other women who God allows to wear pants. Do what God has told you, and don't worry about others.

June 30

Do you always feel the need to be right? Do you insist that your way of doing things is the right way to do things? Do you gloat and boast when you are found to be right? If so, repent and ask God to forgive and deliver you. It doesn't matter whether or not a person is right, it matters only that they ***do*** *what is right at all times. The two are not the same. The need to always be right can lead the Saints of God into a spirit of rebellion. We must concentrate more on doing the right thing, and less on being right. Get right church and let's go home.*

July 1

Have not I commanded thee? Be strong and of a good courage; be not afraid, neither be thou dismayed: for the Lord thy God is with thee wherever thou goest.
Joshua 1:9

Tough love is when we are allowed to hit rock bottom, with seemingly no way out, just to come to the understanding that If God doesn't deliver us from this bondage, no one can. At some point all parents have to use tough love with their children when they are determined to go down a path of destruction. It's hard, but necessary for growth. That's why it is called tough love. God uses this same technique with us when He sees us headed for destruction. When we stop trying to make things possible in our own strength we can totally submit to God.

July 2

To be devoted to Jesus Christ, we need the power of the Holy Spirit. A devoted Christian is no longer concerned with their reputation of what people say or think of them. They are not ashamed to go all the way in everything God commands of them. They are not afraid to be coined as "Jesus freaks" as the unbelieving world perceives. Devoted Christians to causes are everywhere, but devoted Christians to Jesus Christ are rare.

July 3

Perhaps we don't spend a lot of time in the presence of the Lord because we don't want to be confronted with the specific sins that are in our lives. If we repent of all sins but do not delve into the specific sins (naming them one by one), that hinder our spirits, then God can't purge us of what we haven't confessed. To ensure that we repent thoroughly, our prayer should be "Lord cleanse me from my secret faults."

July 4

The closer our relationship with God, the further away worrying is in our lives. It is like oil and water, the two just don't mix. Worry is a direct insult to God and the opposite of faith. God is all powerful, all knowing and forever present. He is totally in control and the Creator of all. So what is there for us to worry about when we are His children?

July 5

Lord God, how many times have I been guilty of entering into situations that were not chosen by You? I would find myself crying out to God in distress and perplexity. God's Word says "in all our ways to acknowledge Him and He will direct our paths." Lord please help me to always put you first in all of my decisions and plans. If it is not what You want for me, help me to obediently walk away.

July 6

Lord God,
help me to obey the Spirit of God in my life. Help me God to practice in my physical being what You have given me by Your Spirit. I have to work out my salvation in everyday practical living. This can be a difficult task because the flesh wars against the Spirit, and the Spirit against the flesh. Only God can deliver me from this wretched state. Thank You God for delivering me.

July 7

"For those who live according to the flesh (what I want, I think and I feel) set their minds on the things of the flesh, but those who live according to the Spirit (Gods word, will and way), the things of the Spirit. For to be carnally (fleshly) minded is death, but to be spiritually minded is life and peace. Because the carnal mind is enmity (opposition) against God; for it is not subject (obedient) to the law of God nor indeed can be. So then those who are in the flesh cannot please God." Are you operating in the flesh or by the Holy Spirit? Is God pleased?

July 8

Prayer Break:

Lord God, please forgive me and deliver me from being a busy body. I have been trying to make it my business to find out where You are leading me. I know my job is to obey You and fully trust You. Lord God, You do not have to explain Yourself or Your plans to me, because You alone are God, not me. "We know in part so we prophecy in part…" I promise to be loyal to You and Your revealed truth and direction for my life. Lord help me not to make up my own plans along the way, whenever I am unaware of how You are moving.

July 9

Praise Break:

My God is so awesome and I truly love and worship Him with my whole heart. Hallelujah to the great I Am, Lord of Lords, and King of Kings. Worthy, Worthy, Worthy, is the Lord God Almighty. From this day forward, I deliberately commit to let You Lord God, be unto me, all that Your Word has promised to those who trust and obey You. I Thank You and I love You. In Your precious Son's name, Jesus Christ, Amen."

July 10

It is unfortunate, but some Christians have come to the faith because of God's retirement benefits. God is wise, and will not be fooled by those who are not truly His servants, but are imposters. The Bible is clear regarding the fate of such people in Luke chapter 13. Many will come to God and profess all the works they performed and signs given by them, but He will say "Depart from Me you workers of iniquity, I know you not."

July 11

Some never come to the full realization of God's Power and Glory and Jesus' work on the Cross. They do not fully and completely surrender their lives over to God. It is as if they are trying to work for their salvation by performing deeds or saying, "I'm a nice person, I have a good heart, I believe people are basically good or I can believe in what I want as long as it doesn't hurt anyone. Wrong! Without the redemptive blood of Jesus, His grace and mercy, we will not see God and will not lead anyone else to Him either.

July 12

Christian Character is on trial. The world is anxiously waiting to give a guilty plea to all who profess to be a Christian, then stumble and fall short of God's glory. No one is perfect, so I don't know why non-Christians (and other Christians), expect us to be perfect. This is why we became Christians, because Jesus was and is perfect and in Him we are redeemed. Christians subscribe to a high standard of moral and ethical beliefs (the Bible). We aren't proclaiming to have a perfect walk with God, but to mature and grow in His grace.

July 13

A lot of schools teach character education (respect, responsibility, kindness, honesty, etc.) to students and incorporate them into curriculum. Students are encouraged to demonstrate these traits for use in self development as well as when interacting with others. The Bible is the authority on character education. If we could establish this fact in our schools and government systems, we would really put into action the motto that this great Country was founded upon and once lived by: "In God we trust."

July 14

Lord Jesus please forgive each of us for not exhibiting the Son of God when faced with insults and misrepresentations. When we are insulted or offended, we must resist the notion to retaliate, but use it as an opportunity to display Christ like behavior. Most of us have so much growing to do in this area in our lives. We have to have faith and pray each day for God to help us and deliver us from the temptation to revile (use abusive language) one another. Let the Lord God bridle our tongues and guard our minds.

July 15

As you reflect over your spiritual walk with Christ, ask yourself; "Have I been doing more than I have been trusting?" Many of us, if we are honest with ourselves have been doing something to help our situations out, instead of trusting God to work them out, in His time and in His way. When money is low, we try to borrow it or find extra sources of income. Rarely do we stand still and trust God to make a way or provide a miracle. When will we learn that God doesn't need our help?

July 16

Do you really understand that only what we do for Christ will last? It doesn't matter much the platform that we serve God through; i.e. jobs, family, community, church, or politics. But it does matter the motivation we have for serving. If we are motivated to serve for money, prestige, honor, fame or glory, then none of that work will last when standing before God at judgment time. However, if our motivation comes from wanting to honor, please, and serve God, then we will hear Him say; "well done, My good and faithful servant."

July 17

"I owe you me Lord." Each saved individual owes Christ their entire life, (not just what they do on Sunday and mid-week service), to use as He sees fit. Our prayers should cease being selfishly motivated and self centered. They need to be dedicated to interceding for others, especially lost souls. Our salvation should have fruits from the harvest of laboring in God's field of spreading the Gospel to the ends of the earth. "The harvest is plenty but the laborers are few."

July 18

How can we know the mind of God, the voice of God, the will of God? By praying, studying, reading and meditating upon the Word of God. We have to model Jesus' example and get away from all the distractions and noise of our everyday lives so we can really focus on God's Word and be able to hear from Him. The voice of God is calling each of us to an intimate relationship with God the Father, the Son and the Holy Spirit. Will you answer the call?

July 19

Even in our witnessing to others about the Gospel, we must be careful that we do not become a traitor to Jesus Christ. It is the Gospel preached that leads to the redemption of souls, not who preaches it or where it is preached. The preacher is only a representative of God, not a god. We allow the enemy access to destroy the work of the Gospel when we exalt people, agendas, gifts, and talents, above the Word of God. Christ must be lifted up to draw all men unto Him. If individuals or doctrines are lifted, then salvation is stifled.

July 20

The Bible clearly says that all disobedience is sin, and it also says "to him who knows to do what is right but does not do what is right, to him that is sin." It is not a natural instinct for humans to obey laws of any kind, whether made by God or manmade, i.e., (speed limits). Most of us at some point, want to do what we want to do, when we want to do it, and how we want to do it. If this mentality were permitted, society would be total anarchy and chaotic to say the least. God's laws are to benefit us not prohibit us and they are always fair, even when men aren't.

July 21

God is so gracious, gentle, and loving that He draws us to Him with His love and kindness. He never demands or forces us to love Him, it is our choice. He is full of compassion and mercy toward all of His creation. I thank God for His long suffering and patience He has shown and given each one of us. The only response that we should have toward God is total obedience and adoration, while praising and thanking Him for salvation, deliverance, healing, restoration and reconciliation.

July 22

Prayer Break:

"Lord God, I want and desire to have an inner exhilaration that is continuous within my spirit. I long for a thirst that only the Holy Spirit can quench. Lord, I want to be in total agreement with and on one accord with Your Spirit and not my flesh. Lord God, Your Word tells us that those who are in the flesh cannot please God. I want to please God. I pray that You mortify (kill), my flesh daily that my spirit may be one with Your Spirit. In Jesus' name I thank You Lord, Amen."

July 23

There is a saying that "when the student is ready, the teacher will appear." We have to remember when witnessing to unbelievers, it is necessary that they see Christ their Savior before they can proceed any further with Him. If unbelievers don't know Jesus as their Savior, His teachings will have little to no meaning for them. Until the Lord draws them into a relationship, they are clueless to Him and His ways. Therefore, the believer's constant prayer is for God to open the eyes of those blind to Jesus Christ as Savior.

July 24

Prayer Break: "Lord Jesus, please hear my prayer and know my spirit, when I ask of You to reconcile and revive me back into a real relationship with You. I desire to be sanctified wholly unto You with no selfish ambitions or motives. Restore and replenish my prayer life, fasting life, praise and worship. Lord God, please forgive me for backsliding in my spirit, even while still attending church services, doing church work, and fellowshipping with church goers. In Jesus' name I pray, Amen."

July 25

The Bible tells us that 'the heart is desperately wicked above all and who can know it", except the Lord, for He knows all things. And again it says "Keep your heart with all diligence, for out of it flows the issues of life." In other words, we need to trust God and His proven word, not our feelings and emotions. For a true believer, the choice to trust God over our feelings can mean life or death, both spiritually as well as physically. No matter what comes our way, we must trust God solely.

July 26

Lord make me over. I desire to be right and pure in my living, motives, dreams, and in the recesses of my mind. I understand that this requires a state of existence that is only possible through a right relationship with Jesus Christ and the power of the Holy Ghost. "If any man be in Christ Jesus, he is a new creature, old things have passed away, behold all thing have become new."

July 27

Disobedience to God is the lethal weapon for spiritual stagnation in the life of a believer. Partial obedience is total disobedience. I think we forget that principle. Just like a woman cannot be a little pregnant, she either is or isn't. The same is true with God, we can't be obedient on some things in some ways. We either obey or disobey, it is just that simple. It never matters our intentions, just our actions. "A little leaven leavens the whole lump."

July 28

"If you are willing and obedient, you shall eat the good of the land." After obedience, comes the promises of God, never vice versa. We can never expect God to manifest His promises to us, if we are disobedient to the Word of God. It would be like rewarding a child for doing the exact opposite of what you told them to do. We are to obey the commands of God for our benefit and well being, not His. It is a sacrifice at times, but it is well worth it.

July 29

It is very interesting to view the trials that we experience as God wanting us to "unlearn" something verses to "teach" us something. The same view can be used to parallel punishment versus discipline. Punishment is always a negative action or response used to modify behaviors or attitudes where as discipline is always a constructive and teachable experience used to grow, nurture or correct behavior and attitudes. Trials are discipline not punishment.

July 30

I believe that all of us at some point and on some level like to operate in the arena of disillusion because then, we can post pone reality. It isn't healthy, useful, or wise to operate in disillusion. It takes a strong, continuous faith in a loving and all powerful God to face reality. When we know who holds our future, then we no longer have to be disillusioned about reality. Because the reality is, we have the victory in Jesus and have already won. Life doesn't have to be filled with disillusion, give yours to Jesus and let Him calm your fears.

July 31

Prayer Break:

"I rebuke the spirit of slothfulness (untidy, messy, careless in work or appearance), in and over my life. I will become spotless and blameless before God in all areas of my life with the help of the Holy Spirit. I surrender my mind, body, and soul to the Lord God to be used as an earthen vessel of honor. As I surrender spiritually to the working of the Holy Spirit in my life, I know that the natural manifestation will soon follow. In Jesus' name, I thank You Lord, Amen."

August 1

What does it mean for a Christian to wait on the Lord? It means to serve the Lord with our total mind, body, and soul. We are to let God's perfect will be done in our lives, without murmuring and complaining. We must serve the Lord in times of joy or sorrow, feeling good or bad, when we have money in our pockets and when we are broke, when we understand His way and when we don't have a clue. Serve the Lord with gladness.

August 2

Thanks be to God for His strength, which is made perfect in weakness. As God brings us through this Christian journey, our daily, hourly, and sometimes by the minute prayer needs to be "Lord give me strength." God will always strengthen His saints. No matter how physically strong we may be, it profits us nothing without God giving us His Spiritual strength to make it through another minute, day, week, month or year. The Lord is the strength of my life.

August 3

It is such an awesome blessing and wonderful thing to know that God has chosen us to bestow His love upon, and we had nothing to do with the choosing. We are so special to God that He personally chose us by name before we were even born. We had no choice as to what natural family we were born into, but we do have to make a choice whether or not we will accept being adopted into the family of God through Jesus Christ. The choice is now up to us, eternal life or eternal damnation.

August 4

Coming to the end of oneself or will, is where we begin our Christian lifestyle of walking, talking, living, and breathing. It is the beginning of a new relationship with God. His will becomes the focus of our lives, not our own agenda, works, talents, or gifts. Only when we give up and give out to our flesh and emotions, can God get us up and moving in His Spirit. It is only in God that we live and move and have our being.

August 5

"Many are called, but few are chosen." Is this because we refuse to answer the call? Do we answer the call but then put the call on hold intending to get back to it later? Or do we just miss the call because we didn't even hear it? Whatever the reason, I pray that God will call again. We need to be waiting with bated breath to not only answer the call, but to fulfill the call as well.

August 6

*Prayer is communication with God, a time to focus solely on being intimate with Him. Intimacy is the focus, not having a long wish list of things for God to do. It is a time to be one with the **ONE** who created all things. We shouldn't be intimidated by prayer time. We must begin to make prayer a priority in our Christian walk. Purposeful prayers are powerful prayers. Pray with the purpose of knowing God on a more intimate level.*

August 7

If we listen we will hear God loud and clear. The Holy Spirit leads and guides the believer every step of this faith walk. But, unfortunately, we don't always follow His leading. Something tells you to help your co-worker out when her hands are full, buy a neighbor some food, or offer free babysitting services for a single parent. These are all examples of the Holy Spirit speaking and leading us. See, I told you that you could hear the Holy Spirit, but now it is up to you to follow His lead.

August 8

During our prayer times, are we allowing the Holy Spirit to make intercessions for us? Are we letting the Spirit give us groanings and utterances that we may not consciously understand? Or do we try to instruct the Holy Spirit on how to operate in our lives accompanied with begging, murmuring and complaining? Jesus sits at the right hand of God to make intercession for us, not to receive instructions from us. Jesus is praying for us, even when we aren't praying for ourselves, or one another.

August 9

Common sense says; don't quit your job until you have another one. The word of God says, "Trust in the Lord with all your heart and He shall direct your steps." Nothing about God or how He operates is ever "common." We cannot try to make "sense" of Him, for His ways are not our ways and His thoughts are not our thoughts. It is a blessing to have common sense, and we should use it wisely. However, being led by the Spirit of God is an awesome, mighty and supernatural adventure.

August 10

The right tool for the job gets the work complete with any project. A builder can't use a hammer to unscrew a door hinge; neither can you use a saw to hang up dry wall. Every tool has a specific use that God allowed man to create it for. So it is with you and me, God has created us to perform specific assignments in building His Kingdom. Only the Master architect has the blueprints to the final project so we can never build anything without Him. As His tools, God knows which of us to use for each project.

August 11

When you are at your wits end, worried, wondering why or why not, wishing for a sign or clue; remember, we walk by faith, not sight. Those who wait on the Lord will renew their strength and mount up with wings like eagles. Once our flesh is exhausted with our own tactics, then God's wisdom will be able to operate in us. As with a person who is drowning, once they have exhausted all of their strength and energy in trying to save themselves and are weak, can they be saved and rescued?

August 12

There is a saying in the world, "I trust you as far as I can see you." Sadly, this is also the faith mentality for many Christians. We trust God as long as we can see how things will work out. But, when we can't see how situations will turn out or work out, we begin to doubt God and wonder if He ***can*** *work everything out. God's abilities should never be judged or questioned based on our inability to figure or help Him work out a situation.*

August 13

How many of us live off of memories? We are stuck in the past, for whatever reason, at a time that we believe "was the best time of our lives." God never looks back and says "those were the days." No, not our eternal God, for He declares in Isaiah 43:18-19 that we forget the past and behold the new things He shall do. The past is behind us, the future with God is ever before us and each day we are here in Him is a gift from God, which we call the **present**. What are we doing each day to please God with our gift of the present?

August 14

Sometimes (a few times a week for some of us), we feel like giving up and quitting. We feel like quitting our jobs, families, and yes, even our spiritual walk with God. As we contemplate giving up, we should always remember that despite our present circumstance, God is good, faithful, kind, longsuffering, a way maker, healer, deliverer, present help in trouble, always on time, father, mother, doctor, lawyer, friend and the lover of our souls. In a nutshell He is above all, in all and works through all. Wow, who can walk away from all that!

August 15

When we seek signs, and evidence from God, to prove who He is, then we have become blind. We are not to chase after signs and wonders, but signs and wonders are to chase us. When we seek His face, obey His word, worship Him in Spirit and Truth, set ourselves apart for holiness and sanctification; then we can see Him, hear Him, feel His presence and be used by Him in mighty ways, beyond our imagination. God will get the glory for the marvelous things He has done, will do and is doing in our lives, not us.

August 16

Prayer Break:

"Lord God, I know and can quote scriptures, I know and can sing spiritual songs, and I have been in many church services, revivals, and conferences. But if I don't know You intimately for me, all else is in vain and useless. If my memory fails me of scriptures, my voice fails to sing a tune, or if I can't get to a church service, none of these things should be able to severe my relationship with You Lord God if I know You intimately. In You I live, move and have my being, in Jesus' name, Amen."

August 17

It is so heart breaking to me when God shows me "ME" and I see myself through Him and His Word. I realize that I don't have it all together and I have missed the mark yet again. I know that when He shows me my fallen state, it is not to deter, depress, or destroy me, but to get me back on track and in line with His Word. I need to repent, obey, be still, cry out to Him then turn from the wrong doings He has revealed to me. These things must be done if I am to be used by God as a vessel of honor not dishonor.

August 18

I really love the Lord and am thankful for His redemptive work on the Cross. Now, do I understand God all the time and how He chooses to operate in my life? No of course not. But God hasn't called me to always understand Him, but He has called me to always obey Him. Obedience to God doesn't always require understanding on my part, but it does always require sacrifice on my part. Understanding that God is in total control involves the willingness to sacrificially obey Him.

August 19

Lord please teach me to rest in You, totally and completely without wavering and doubting. Resting in the Lord God demands faith. Doubting and wavering comes from fear. Faith is of God, fear is from the devil. Perfect love (which is God), casts out fear. I know that God is the same yesterday, today and forever, so if He healed me, set me free and delivered me before, then He is more than able to do it again, and again, and again, and again…

August 20

It is the sick person who really values and knows what health is; it is the blind person who values and knows what sight is; the deaf person who knows and appreciates hearing; the lame who appreciates walking and the poor who appreciates wealth. Those who are lost in sin know they are lost and don't need us to judge them for being lost. They do need Jesus preached and displayed in our lives. He draws us all with love and kindness. Those who are well have no need of a physician; Jesus came to save that which was lost.

August 21

Those who have positively influenced us did so by God's divine interaction, not by their own accord. When we set out to be an influence, we are relying on our own abilities. When we rely on God's abilities and focus our efforts on glorifying God, it produces a greater influence on people whom we may scarcely remember coming into contact with. When our goal is to please God, not man, we leave a trail of God inspired circumstances along the way.

August 22

"For the joy that was set before Him, He endured the cross." We know what all was involved with Jesus going to the cross, (His crucifixion), but what was the joy that was set before Him? Could it be a family reunion? Could this be the way God would reconcile us back to Him? YES! Jesus endured the Cross so that He could have His family restored back to God the Father. As Christians, we should be so grateful that Jesus died and rose again so that we may also die to Him in our flesh, but reign with Him in eternity.

August 23

"Okay Lord, I'm down here on my knees to pray, now what?" Prayer can seem intimidating. Our minds wander, our bodies are tired and distractions seem to constantly prevail. If we could just enter into an instant prayer festival, then everything would be great. Praying takes a mindset of "stick to itivness." It is a purpose of the will; it is not based on conditions. We stay with prayer despite the natural circumstances and we spiritually sell out and give ourselves over to God.

August 24

The battle is the Lords, and He has already won. It is as if we are participating in a fixed fight. The opponent, the devil, is trying his best to make us believe we are defeated, but he is a liar. The Bible tells us that the devil comes to steal, kill and destroy. But Jesus came to give us abundant life. The devil desires to destroy our relationship with God that Jesus paid the price for back on Calvary. When the devil attacks your mind, body or emotions, just remind him of his eternal fate, and then praise God for yours.

August 25

What a friend we have in Jesus, all our sins and grief's to bear, what a privilege it is to carry, EVERYTHING to God in prayer. The words of this hymn are a refuge for Christians everywhere. We have in Jesus, the best friend we could ever imagine, (our BFF). He is a friend that sticks closer than a brother and He laid down His life for us, His friends. With a Friend like Jesus, what can mere man do to us to threaten or harm us? As the Bible says, a three cord bond isn't easily broken, (Jesus, the Holy Spirit, you.)

August 26

He who keeps his mind stayed on Christ Jesus; God will keep that person in perfect peace. What an awesome thing it is to be kept in the perfect peace of God. His peace surpasses everyone's understanding, including our own. The world can't receive God's peace because it can only come from having an intimate relationship with God. There is a bumper sticker that can be seen on cars as they drive around town that is so true to the Christian walk; "No God, No peace, Know God, Know peace."

August 27

"This little light of mine, I'm gonna let it shine, everywhere I go, I'm gonna let it shine, Jesus gave it to me so I'm gonna let it shine, let it shine, let it shine, let it shine." Many of us that profess to be Christians have not been living the words of this song. Our lights have ceased to shine **anywhere** we go; home, work, store, and even church. Jesus is the light of the world and if we abide in Him and His word abides in us, and then we too are the light of the world, all day, and every day, everywhere.

August 28

"Pray without ceasing; pray believing you shall receive; pray one for another; watch therefore and pray that you enter not into temptation; everyone that is Godly shall pray to You in a time when You may be found; if My people who are called by My name would humble themselves and pray, seek My face, turn from their wicked ways, then will I hear from heaven forgive their sins and heal the land." A Christian who doesn't pray, is like a car without gas, even though it looks good, it is useless and will go nowhere.

August 29

"Now faith is the substance of things hoped for, the evidence of things not seen." Therefore, if you can see it, at any angle, then it isn't faith, it is a reality. I don't need faith to pay my bills when I have money in the bank and my income flow is secure and stable. But, when I've lost my job, don't have any money in the bank, can't find any or borrow any money, and the bills are past due, then faith must be activated. Faith says "I trust God and will praise Him for His greatness, knowing He promised to never leave or forsake me."

August 30

When we ask God to use us for His glory, we need to make sure it is for His glory, not our own. It is a dangerous thing to steal God's glory. If God uses you to help someone or to go before powerful and influential people, don't congratulate yourself or boast of your abilities. But glorify God who has blessed you to do these mighty and awesome deeds, then use your gifts and talents to advance His Heavenly Kingdom. Because in the end, only what we do for Christ will last. Heaven and earth will pass away.

August 31

"The joy of the Lord is my strength; weeping may endure for a night, but joy comes in the morning; In God's presence is fullness of joy; those who sow in tears shall reap in joy." In our Christian walk, each of us must have the precious fruit of joy operating in our lives. Joy is one of the nine fruits of the spirits listed in Galatians 5:22-23. Happiness depends on what "happens" and is conditioned by circumstances. But joy is from God and isn't dependent upon what happens, we have it in spite of our circumstances.

But my God shall supply all your need according to his riches in glory by Christ Jesus
Philippians 4:19

September 1

The Bible is very clear; without holiness, no man shall see God; be holy for I am holy. God plainly tells us that He expects us to live a holy lifestyle. However, I am not so sure that many who profess to be Christians believe God. A lot of Christians can be found saying "it doesn't take all of that to serve God; God knows my heart; I go to church, I believe in God…" The devil is a liar; it does take all that and more, to truly live a holy and consecrated life before God and man.

September 2

A beautiful glass of our favorite beverage or a succulent meal can be pleasing to the eye. However, it can neither satisfy our thirst nor fill our hunger to merely gaze upon them. The beverage and the food must be used to truly satisfy and be purposeful. So it is with Christians, we are not to be merely adorned with precious jewels, extravagant clothes, nice cars and homes just to show off the blessings of the Lord. But Christians are to be used by God in some of the most undesirable situations to show the Glory of God and His Kingdom.

September 3

Let's understand something; God never blesses us physically, financially, or spiritually for us to hoard the blessings to ourselves. God blesses us so that we may be a blessing to others. We are to share our blessings with those God puts in our paths. Just as food and water are not just for the satisfaction of the mouth and stomach, but the entire body needs them to sustain life. The same is true with the body of Christ. The blessings received by one Christian will help to sustain the whole body of believers.

September 4

Have you ever gone to see your favorite action hero movie? Was it Superman, Spiderman or Batman? You knew the hero would win at the end, even up against seemingly stronger and wiser villains than himself, and up to the point of death. It is always eventful and sometimes tense. Well our Christian walk is the same. We know we win in the end, but along the way we face many villains and sometimes feel like we are at the brink of death. Our journey is always eventful, and sometimes tense, but in the end we win.

September 5

Watch as well as pray! Watch for little cracks and crevices that the enemy uses as entrances into our lives. Watch out for gossiping, unforgiveness, jealousy, dishonesty, pride, idolatry, rebellion… We have to ask God to grant us more discernment in spotting the traps of the enemy. The devil can never be underestimated or his plans to kill, steal, or destroy, taken lightly. As long as we play church and not exert any real power over the enemy or engage in spiritual warfare, the enemy can run rampant. Let us be about our Fathers' work.

September 6

I marvel at people who seem to super naturally take irritable people and situations and produce pearls. Maybe the grocery store clerk is rude and obnoxious at the checkout lane, and then they remarkably disarm the rudeness with tact and sincerity leaving behind an apologetic cashier. This is a gift of God because our normal nature is to fight fire with fire. But as Jesus showed us while dying on the Cross at Calvary; "Forgive them for they know not what they do."

September 7

I know you realize it is impossible for our natural bodies to live without air, food, and water, but do you realize that this refers to our spiritual lives as well? When our natural bodies don't get these three things, we eventually die. The same is true for our spirits. God is the breath of life, the bread of heaven and the river of life. God breathed and man became a living soul, God provided manna from heaven for the children of Israel and the water that God will give us shall be as a well of water.

September 8

As born again Christians, we are set free from the bondage of sin. However, our flesh is not saved and can never be, that is why God will give us a new body in eternity. Daily we must kill the flesh with its evil lusts and desires because it opposes the spirit man in each of us. God's Word says "no flesh will tarry in his presence". To see God, serve God, know God and worship God, it must all be done in the spirit. God is a spirit and those of us who worship God must worship Him in spirit and truth.

September 9

Being led by the Spirit is not dancing and shouting all over the sanctuary, or keeping track of all you do to help for a "good works" marathon. It is being sensitive and in tune with the voice of God and subject to His divine will. And just how does that happen? It happens through quality quiet time with God in prayer, bible study, fasting, and worship. It also calls for a made up mind to obey God at all costs, in all areas, at all times. In essence, it requires that we decrease so that Christ may increase.

September 10

No one prepares for a storm during a hurricane or tornado. No one prepares for battle during the war. And no one prepares an evacuation plan during a fire. Those important preparations are devised and rehearsed during times of peace. So why is it then that many Christians choose to pray, worship and seek God during the trial but not before or after it has passed? It is obvious they aren't prepared so they get blind sighted. Let's learn to stay spiritually prepared for attacks from the enemy by having a continuous prayer and worship life.

September 11

God's love, kindness, grace and mercy are without limits. The Bible tells us that with love and kindness God draws each of us to Him. We were led to Christ by kindness not condemnation. While we were yet sinners, (still in sin, doing our own thing), Christ died for us. He didn't wait for us to get ourselves together, stop drinking, drugging, lying, cheating, or committing unlawful sexual acts to give His life for ours. His mercy endures forever and He doesn't get tired of us, and we should never get tired or tire out on Him.

September 12

When our faith is under attack, we have to hold on to the word and promises of God even tighter, with both hands. God is faithful even when we are not. It may seem like our whole world is colliding together, but remember that God is always in control and He will never give us more than we can handle or bare. So we must continue, no matter how we feel, to seek God, praise Him, serve Him, and worship Him even when our faith is under attack.

September 13

To surrender to the will of God is to surrender YOUR will. It is no longer, "I want, I think, I need, I feel", but "Lord, whatever You want, say, or need." This way of living can be difficult to attain, in our own strength, but we can do all things through Christ who strengthens us. We believe we can help God out by doing our own things. Not true, it never works. We need to tell God "I want to please You , I need to obey Your word, I feel the pain and suffering of the Cross and when I think of all You have done, my soul says Hallelujah."

September 14

You're lost, you're confused, you're worried, you're anxious, you're tired and you want to give up and give out. This is a trick of the enemy, don't believe his lies. "Stand still and see the salvation of the Lord; My God shall supply all of your needs according to His riches in Christ Jesus; Yes, though I walk through the valley of the shadow of death, I will fear no evil;" God is near to those who call upon Him and will give you peace that surpasses all understanding. Blindly trust God to work things out that your 20/20 vision can't see at the moment.

September 15

Repent for any and all sins that you may have committed knowingly and unknowingly. Repent for the kingdom of God is at hand. Ask God to reveal everything that may be hindering your walk with Him; (unforgiveness from childhood wounds, gossip, dishonesty, deceit, ungodly thoughts, etc.) Repent, forgive, and let God heal and deliver you so that you will be able to go on in victory. Leave all concerns, issues and problems with God, these things were never meant to be carried by you anyway.

September 16

As a Christian, do you have a prayer life; a fasting life; a worshiping spirit; a giving spirit? As soldiers in the army of the Lord, these are very important weapons and resources needed to fight this spiritual battle. The weapons of our warfare are not carnal (guns, knives, revenge, back biting, gluttony, bullying, violence, etc), but are mighty through God to the pulling down of strong holds (generational curses, demonic activities). Praying, worshiping God, fasting, and giving are effective battlefield weapons that each Christian must possess!

September 17

The devil uses temptations to get us out of the will of God. However, temptation is not sin, it is merely an invitation to disobey God, and disobedience is sin. If you accept the invitation of temptation, you have sinned against God and heaven. If you resist the temptation and run the other direction, then you have received the victory over that temptation. God doesn't tempt us, but He does test the heart and mind of man, to reveal to us where we really are in our Christian walk and show us how much we need to rely on His grace and mercy, not works.

September 18

Let's get one thing straighten out; the devil is not after your gifts and talents nor your houses and cars. The devil doesn't want your choir solo, your townhouse, or your S.U.V. The devil is after your faith (without which, no man or woman can please God) and he is after your character (who you are when no one is paying attention). If the devil can get you to doubt the Word and promises of God, and display ungodly character, then he has tempted you to sin, you accepted it, acted on it, sinned and believed his lies.

September 19

Blessed are the man and woman who don't walk in the counsel or advice of the ungodly person. The ungodly are like the chaff (worthless matter) that the wind blows away they will not stand in judgment time but shall perish. The blessed person delights in the Lord's law and meditates in His word day and night. They are rooted and grounded and whatever the blessed person does, it will prosper. We have to make a conscious choice to live a prosperous and blessed godly life, not a chaffed, cursed ungodly life. Don't let the devil blow you away.

September 20

Character- who you are when no one is watching. Integrity-Godly values and morals you practice and live. Faith-what and who you put your trust in. Compassion-sincere, genuine concern for others. Obedience- unwavering devoted loyalty to laws, commands, and authority. Love-the sacrificial giving of yourself to benefit others. If you are a Christian (Christ like), are these apart of your daily walk with Christ? Do others see these attributes displayed by you, especially the lost?

September 21

The Christian identity is to bear the image and likeness of God Himself; our goal is not to be good, but to be like God (as little gods). We need to be forgiving, faithful, giving, patient, and love sinners (but hate sin). A person who is focusing on being good is trying to please people. A Godly person only seeks to please God and obey Him. A person who focuses on being good seeks after happiness, the love of life and approval of others. A Godly person knows that their Christian journey must mirror the life, death, and resurrection of Christ.

September 22

Guess what? God created us, we didn't create Him! We are made to bless the Lord, not for God to solely bless us (which He does freely anyway). We are created to give God the glory, not steal His glory (my gifts, my talents, my abilities, mine, mine, mine…). We are made to worship the Giver of all gifts that He blesses us to enjoy, not to worship the gift (house, mate, kids, job, car, etc). We are created to obey the voice of God, not have God do what we want or think He should do in our lives. The creation can't control the Creator!

September 23

Jesus Christ is the Son of God, not His servant. However, Jesus did obey every command of His Father, like a faithful Servant. But now we are God's servants and Jesus is the mediator between us and God. We are able to pray to God directly through the work of Jesus on the Cross. The Son came to do the will of His Father. The Father was well pleased with Jesus. Jesus served us by preaching the good news of the Gospel. We serve God by obeying His word and spreading the Gospel everywhere. We are joint heirs with Jesus Christ the Son of God.

September 24

The goal of every Christian should be to do God's will. Do you know God's will for your life? If not, have you sought after God to find out His will for your life? Are you doing God's will that He has called for your life? If not, what hindrances have you allowed to keep you from doing God's will in your life? What action steps can you put into place to begin or grow further in God's will for your life? Remember that the will of God will never take you where the grace of God will not keep you.

September 25

Please know and understand that there is nothing hidden from God. Nothing we say, do or even think is ever hidden from the omnipotent God of our souls. On the other hand, there are things within us that are hidden from us that only God himself can reveal to us (selfishness, greed, hatred, etc). Ask God to reveal any secret things that may be hidden in you that need to come out so you can grow further in your spiritual walk with the Lord. "Lord if there is anything in me that should not be, take it out and strengthen me, Amen."

September 26

Have you ever noticed that some of the things that God has called us to do or become, commissioned us to carry out or perform are not easily done by us in the natural (of our own ability or knowledge)? God gave us His grace to accomplish the things He asks of us so that we know without a doubt that God is in control, not us. All the glory, honor, and praise will go to Him not us. When others try to give us His glory or puff us up, we will correct them and say "No it was God using me."

September 27

Reconciliation is to be put back together in a right relationship with another party after having been separated by a dispute or wrong doing. Jesus' death reconciled mankind back to God the Father after Adam's sin. All who accept Jesus' work on the Cross and repent of sins are restored back to a right relationship with God. Thank you Jesus! Now, is there anyone here on earth that you need to be reconciled with? Who do you need to forgive for doing you wrong or who have you done wrong and need to ask them for forgiveness?

September 28

The Bible tells us that when we come to the church alter and ask God to forgive us, if while there, we remember that we need to be forgiven by others, or forgive someone, then leave the alter at once and be reconciled to our brother or sister. If God loved us enough to sacrifice His only Son Jesus, to have His family restored back to Himself, then surely we can sacrifice our need to be right at the expense of gaining our brothers and sisters back to us. Let's cancel the pity party and show love, forgiveness and compassion toward others.

September 29

The Word of God (the Holy Bible), is the standard for all who profess Christ as Lord and Savior of their lives. It is not an option or suggestion of things you could try, it is the epitome of what Christians should strive to do, how they should live and what commands to obey every day, not just on Sundays and Holidays. Yes, the standard is high, but the reward of eternal life is worth any temporary inconveniences that may arise in the flesh. God tells us that His grace is sufficient for us to make it through. God will never let us down.

September 30

"God is good all the time, and all the time, God is good." This may sound like a cliché', but when you stop and think about all God has done for you and your family, the only response is that God is good. God draws us close to Him with His loving and kind ways. He doesn't beat us into a relationship with Him, or make us love Him, serve Him, or obey Him. God lets us choose Him. He loves us unconditionally, watches over us, and provides for us, even before we ever gave our lives to Him. And He does all this because He is a good God.

October 1

Pride goes before destruction and a haughty spirit (loftiness or high minded), before a fall. The demonic spirit of pride can and will destroy lives if left unchecked to fester and grow. It may seem subtle at first (I did great, I'm really good etc.), but before long it can become unbearable to those who come into contact with it. Repent of any and all prideful spirits and ask God to deliver and set you free, even if you don't think it is an issue in your life. Repent because you never know what seeds may be trying to germinate in your heart.

October 2

Prayer break:

"Lord God, please deliver me from me! Please cleanse me from my secret faults. Purge me with hyssop and deliver me from all evil, lustful and prideful thoughts. Lord God please deliver me from gossiping, murmuring, complaining, disobedience, rebellion, selfishness, stubbornness, self-righteousness and hypocrisy. Lord set me free from sins known and unknown. I surrender to the will of God and I thank You for my deliverance, in Jesus Christ name, Amen."

October 3

Why did God save us from sin? Was it because we deserved or worked for it? Was it to go to church every Sunday and mid-week service to sing, pray, and hear the word of God then go back home as if nothing had happened during service? I pray that is not the gist of our walk with Christ. Could it be that God saved us to not just serve Him in church but to also be a light to a dark and dying world? Did God save us so the ungodly could get a glimpse of the transformation power of Jesus Christ, then desire the same? I pray this is what we are doing.

October 4

Please be aware that the devil is a liar and he comes to steal, kill and to destroy you. Don't be intimidated by his tactics because he is already defeated and is jealous of you and your relationship with God. So when the devil tells you that you will never be anything, God would never love and accept you after what you have done, nobody wants you around; just laugh at him and say "Ha! That is your destiny not mines! I am the apple of Gods eye, and He loves me so much that He gave His only Son to die for me, in my place."

October 5

The most basic definition of sin is- I am my own god. That was the devil's viewpoint that got him cast out of heaven. It was also the viewpoint he planted in the mind of Eve to get her to eat the fruit, who then got her husband to join her. And it is the viewpoint sinners consistently have about their lives and who they obey and submit to (themselves/their flesh). And unfortunately it is sometimes the viewpoint used to get the saints of God to sin and disobey Gods known truths (surely God didn't mean…) yes He Did!

October 6

God will never save a person from their sins unless the person asks God to save and deliver them. God will not force Himself, His love, grace, mercy or redemption on anyone. God lets us choose to accept Him or not. God lovingly displays His awesome character and attributes for us to either embrace or reject. But understand that God never rejects us no matter how "bad off" someone may think they are or we may think they are. Remember that Gods arm is not too short to reach down to the lowest pits and save a willing soul.

October 7

If God is the same yesterday, today, and forever, that means that He never changes. If God never changes, then that means that He is faithful and true. If He is faithful and true that means God never fails. If God never fails and you put your trust in Him, especially during the valley times of your life, then that means you can never fail as long as you trust and obey God. Trust and obedience go together. God says that His sheep know His voice and a stranger they will not follow. Ask yourself whose voice are you following, Gods, yours, or the devils'.

October 8

There is a statement people say which goes "some people are so heavenly bound that they are no earthly good." In other words, they are so focused on getting to heaven that they use it as a fire protection plan to avoid going to hell. The Christians responsibility is not making it to heaven, because acceptance and belief of the salvation work of Jesus Christ does that all by itself. Christians are to be wise and win souls. In other words live an earthly life that makes others want to meet Jesus face to face and serve Him with their entire life.

October 9

God hates sin, but He loves the sinner. Sin separates us from God. He can't look upon sin because God is Holy. Jesus Christ bore our sins on the Cross in order to restore mankind back to a righteous relationship with God our Father. God sowed His only begotten Son in order to reap a family. One life given, to restore all lives for all who would accept the redemptive work of the Cross. In the natural world this sheds a whole new light on the statement of one person can make a difference. What a difference Christ makes in our lives.

October 10

If we could really grasp the understanding of just how much God loves us and only wants to give us His best in every part of life, I don't think we would rebel against Him the way we do. God is a loving Father who wants to protect us from harm, heal all our diseases, provide for our every need and give us the desires of our hearts. God is the best Dad Ever! Satan also knows this and sends attacks everyday to get us to do as Job's wife said "curse God and die" But we must have the patience of Job and the faith of Abraham.

October 11

As sanctified and holy as we may be in our walk with God; as pure and faithful as we may live; as much as we give of ourselves and our resources; in and of ourselves we cannot save anyone from a life of sin and shame. Only God can save souls. We sometimes forget that we didn't save ourselves, it was God. Only God can save our families, friends and co-workers. We can win souls for the Kingdom by our witness, testimony, brotherly love, giving and obedience to God's commands, but ultimately it is God who saves the soul we win.

October 12

You may be at a place where you do not know what to do next, who to go to, or what prayer to pray. You have been fasting and seeking the Lord, giving and serving, so what now? "Stand still and see the salvation of the Lord; Peace be still; be still and know that I am God; God is not the author of confusion; the promises of God in Him are yes and Amen." The silence that comes from God during this time in your life is also your answer from God. When God is ready for you to proceed in a certain direction, He will speak loud and clear.

October 13

We all hate to be ignored, especially when we have a question that we don't know the answer to or how to solve. When God is silent toward us, it is time for us to be still, listen and trust Him. Have you ever noticed that silent and listen are spelled with the exact same letters? Remember when you were a child and asked your parents a question, and they purposely didn't answer but gave you a look that said, "Do not proceed any further, stop right there" and you did? Later when the time was appropriate you got your answer, same with God.

October 14

Praise Break:

Hallelujah, Thank You Jesus, glory to God. We worship You oh Lord. How wonderful and mighty are Your works and this our souls know very well. You are an awesome God and worthy of all the glory, honor and praise. Let everything that has breath praise the living, loving, gracious, merciful, faithful, all knowing and all powerful God. We love You, thank You, and adore You. Worthy is the Lord God almighty of all our praises. How blessed are we to serve such an awesome God.

October 15

There is a great difference between being a Christian and being a spiritual person. We are all spirits who possess a mind and live in a body. But we are not all Christians, Christ like. Christians mirror the image of Christ in obedience, love and character. The only way to serve, worship, and commune with God the Father, who is a spirit, is through Jesus Christ His Son, the mediator between us and God. Christians, be clear about whose you are and know who you represent,
Christ Jesus, our Savior.

October 16

Have you been called by God or chosen by Him to do a specific work in this life? God will equip and qualify you for what He has called you to do. Remember, "God doesn't call the qualified, He qualifies the called". Now here comes the part we never discuss about being called; Training and Discipline by God in the wilderness of life. From called to qualified is a journey filled with trials, disappointments, discouragement, loss, misunderstanding, loneliness, etc. But in the end we know Romans 8:28 works in our favor.

October 17

Lord God, I bind the spirit of deception that is running rampant on the earth these last days. Lord God, reveal Yourself as the Only true and living God. Show mankind that the only viable access to You is through a relationship with Your Son Jesus the Christ. Jesus is the Way, the Truth and the Life, no one comes to God the Father, except through Jesus. Allah, Jehovah, Buddha, Mohamed, Confucius, a higher power, or spiritual guide, etc., none of these names will grant access to the Father. Jesus is the only name given under heaven that can save mankind.

October 18

"Oh the blood of Jesus will never lose its power." The blood has power to save from addictions and lust. Power to heal every kind of sickness and disease. Power to forgive. Power to set free minds and bodies. Power to protect and keep families and friends. Power to provide every need and fulfill every Godly desire. Power to fight adversity, strongholds and spiritual wickedness in high places. Power to love unconditionally . And power to serve and obey every command the Lord God has given in His Word, the Bible.

October 19

There is a saying that prayer is the key, but faith unlocks the door. Have you ever had a key that fit perfectly into a door key hole but it couldn't turn the lock to unlock the door? Well that's how prayer is without faith. It doesn't work. Your faith moves God to turn the prayer keys that unlock doors. "When you pray, believe that you will have what you ask and it shall be given unto you." Prayer and faith co-exist and without the two, you are just locked out of all that God has planned for you.

October 20

"If you love me feed my sheep". Do you really love God? Are you feeding His sheep? If not, why not? If so, how? This verse of scripture doesn't mean you have to physically provide food for others, although that is a godly service. But it does mean that you should be like Christ when He says "I must be about my Father's business." What business is His Father in? Reconciliation! God wants us, His creation, back in covenant relationship with Him. We must feed God's creation the Good News of Jesus' work on the Cross.

October 21

Have you noticed that work days and work weeks are getting longer and worship services or getting shorter? You can sometimes choose from as many as three different Sunday morning worship times? Families are getting smaller and their houses are getting bigger. There is more crime, divorce, sexual misconduct and abuse than ever before. So why hurry home from a 45 minute worship service to a big empty house and prepare for a new six day work week? God deserves more quality time with you. This is not the life God's Word promises for the believer.

October 22

Have you ever loved someone who probably didn't even know you existed (a famous person)? Have you ever loved someone who didn't love you back or rejected your feelings? Have you ever loved someone who didn't deserve your love because they trampled on your heart? It hurts doesn't it? If only they could see how much you want to be there for them, take care of them, support, protect, and give them their hearts desire, then maybe they would love you the way you love them. This is how God feels when we reject His love for us.

October 23

Love's a choice; we choose to love or not love someone. God is love, and wants us to choose to love Him back. God loved us from the beginning; before we knew who He was in our lives. God patiently waits for us to accept His love but He never forces His love upon us. He is a gentle and meek Lover. God loves all of His creation and desires that we love Him in return. We express our love toward God by giving Him praise, worshiping Him, and spending time alone in prayer and Bible study. Get to know Him and obey His commands.

October 24

God rarely calls people who we think are qualified to get a job done. God rarely chooses people who we think look the part, talk the part or look as if they have it all together. If God is calling you to do something in the kingdom and you feel inexperienced or unqualified, then get ready for the adventure of your life. God has already equipped you with everything you need to fulfill the call and purpose He has for you (a total reliance upon Him). Don't be afraid, as He told Moses in Ex 4:10-11, so He is telling you.

October 25

As saints of God we aren't necessarily always called to walk on water, raise the dead or be thrown into a den of lions or fiery furnace, at least not on a daily basis. But we are called to be extraordinary in the ordinary. That takes the grace of God. Much of our saintly lives are filled with ordinary and mundane routines. When doing daily ordinary things, God still requires us to display joy, peace, love, compassion, selflessness, and all the other godly traits modeled by Jesus.

October 26

The blessing of the Lord that makes us rich and adds no sorrow with it isn't houses, cars, spouses, healings, power, fame, etc, these are all Things! So what is the blessing of the Lord? The Lord God Himself! Having a personal, intimate relationship with God is truly the blessing of our life. If God takes away the Things, we sometimes mistake as the blessing, but we still have Him, we are blessed. If we have Things and not God we are cursed, miserable, lonely, empty, lost and forever damned. What will it profit to gain the world and loose our soul?

October 27

Christians are victors perpetually. We live, breathe and move in victory through Jesus Christ. The battle is already won. God declared the end from the beginning. We are more than conquerors through Him who loved us. So serve the devil a notice that he has already been defeated and no weapon he forms against you shall prosper. Take note that he will form weapons against you, but the weapons will not prosper. Greater is He (God) that is in you than he (the devil) who is in the world. Thank God for our victory.

October 28

No matter what your situation looks like, God is in control! God still sits on the throne watching over the good and the bad, the just and the unjust. God sits high and looks low. God is in control of the political systems of the world, the monetary systems of the world, jobs, families and religious orders. Nothing happens on planet earth that He didn't allow to happen, even though He didn't cause it to happen. The prince of the air (the devil) can only go so far because God stops his hand from causing utter destruction.

October 29

Do you know God's will for your life? I do. It is total, complete, and absolute obedience to Him and His Word. This requires total self-sacrifice of your own will and complete trust that God's way is better for you. God created us so it only makes sense that He knows mankind better than we know ourselves. We always want the experts' advice on health, fitness, hair, skin care, cars, homes, investments, etc. Why not obey the expert on mankind, God?

October 30

Do you really believe God is able to perform and keep every promise that He made you? We say we do, but when things look bleak and we can only see darkness ahead, then we allow doubt to set in. Once we begin to have even the slightest trace of doubt, then we are essentially saying God isn't God because "we" can't see how He will do what He said. Never question God's ability to perform based on our impaired vision, doubts and fears. Repent of unbelief.

October 31

The Lord God is worthy to be praised, not because of our situations (bills paid, good health, and peaceful family). But the Lord God almighty is worthy to be praised because of who He is, in spite of our situations (no money, sick, divorce.) God is good all the time, even when times aren't good. God is our anchor, shield, and buckler through the good and the bad, the smooth and the rough times. When we learn to praise God solely because He is worthy, we then become instruments of Praise. Glory Hallelujah!

Before I formed thee in the belly I knew thee; and before thou came forth out of the womb I sanctified thee, and I ordained thee a prophet unto the nations
Jeremiah 1:5

November 1

Faith makes the intangible – tangible and the unseen – appear. The Bible tells us that God has given every man a measure of faith. In other words, we all do believe, just not at the same levels. Some people have great faith, like the centurion soldier and some have little faith like the disciples. Where on the spectrum of great to least does your faith fall? What can you do to grow your faith in God? Remember that without faith it is impossible to please God. When your faith is in action, does it make Gods promises tangible and appear?

November 2

Faith is a lifestyle. We have faith that God is who He says He is and that He will provide for us and keep us. We have faith that He is coming back for us and that we will reign with Him forever. Faith believes God is in control, that He will never leave us nor forsake us and will keep every promise He gave us. Faith is believing, not seeing, but then one day seeing what we believed God for all along (saved family members, healings, deliverance from additions, cars, homes, etc.)

November 3

Alone time with God must be a priority in the life of a believer. Quiet time with God prepares us for the noise of life from work, family, traffic etc. We must set aside time to spend with God in prayer, meditation, bible study, praise, worship and daily devotions. This quiet time with God will train us in building up spiritual strength and stamina needed for each day's journey. If we don't get time to talk with and listen to God, then how will we know His plans for our lives?

November 4

Whatever you are going to be; you already are. Whatever you already are you have always been. The problem lies in the awareness. For example God isn't going to be God He already is and has always been, well before we ever came into the knowledge of Him. Our awareness of or lack of awareness of God doesn't dictate Him being God, He just is. Therefore we that were predestined before the foundation of the world are heirs and joint heirs with Jesus Christ.

November 5

Has God ever taken something away from you that you really wanted, but deep inside you knew it wasn't what God wanted you to have? Maybe it was a certain job, relationship, house or car. Did you throw a tantrum, cry, sulk, or get an attitude when it didn't work out the way you wanted? Repent and tell God you're sorry for the tantrum, then thank God for keeping you from dangers seen and unseen; especially when you didn't want to be kept. Our Heavenly Father always keeps us as the apple of His eye.

November 6

Does this sound familiar, "Lord have Your way in my life, send me I'll go, not my will, but your will be done, Lord use me…?" So when tests and trials come upon you why do you seem surprised and say, "woe is me, why me, I've been faithful." If God is going to use us we have to experience tribulations so we can witness to others about the grace, mercy, love, healing forgiveness… of God. Truthfully the trial was never about you anyway, it was to help someone else along the way who finds themselves where God delivered you from.

November 7

As we face life's trials, disappointments, setbacks and difficult circumstances; the Bible tells us to speak to the mountain (trial) to be removed and cast into the sea. However, most of us speak about how high the mountain is, how rough the side is we are climbing, how we are afraid of heights, etc. We have to stop telling God how big and bad the mountain is and start telling the mountain how big and bad our God is. God has given us authority to bind (tie up the trials) on earth and He will bind (tie up the trials) in Heaven.

November 8

As children of the Most High God, I want you to know that you are admired for who God made you to be. Your family and friends really appreciate the role you share in their lives. You are a gift from God to all who know you. Your loved ones believe in you and are so grateful that you believe in them as well. God has ordained you to be the head and not the tail, first and not last, above and not beneath. So walk with the assurance that God loves you and has made you in His image. You are fearfully and wonderfully made.

November 9

In God's eyes there are only two types of people; those saved by the blood of Jesus and the unsaved who haven't confessed Jesus as Lord of their life. Everybody on the face of the earth fits into one category or the other, there is no in between. We sometimes get so caught up categorizing which of the two areas we think other people fall into that we never really commune with God to see how we measure up to God's standards. God does not send anyone to hell; people go of their own free will for rejecting Christ.

November 10

If you were to die tonight, would you open your eyes up in heaven? If your answer is anything other than YES, then stop right now and repent of any and all sins, ask Jesus to come into your heart and declare Him risen from the dead as Lord and Savior of your life, in Jesus' name Amen. Now your eternity is sealed with God, Jesus and the Holy Spirit. Worshipping and serving the Lord corporately in a bible based church will help with the understanding of living in holiness. Now you never have to worry about your future again!

November 11

Sometimes we put God on our agenda. We say "I have to go to choir rehearsal Thursday, Bible study on Wednesday, and revival on Friday... This attitude is not one of fellowshipping with God, but of duty to religion. God should not be on a list of things to do that can be checked off when completed. Our time with God is never complete it is perpetual. The above things are not wrong actions, but the mindset toward them is warped. When we say things in a "have to" manner, our heart isn't in it. We have become sounding brass and clanging symbols.

November 12

Salvation is the greatest gift that any of us could ever receive. But sadly, so many don't accept it and have become separated from God. The gift of salvation is free, but it does cost. It will cost each individual the right to their own will and way. "Let this mind be in you that was also in Christ Jesus". Jesus had the mind to-do the will of His Father, and so we must. We have to deny ourselves and take up the cross, bear the burdens of the life, death, and resurrection of Jesus Christ. He must increase and we must decrease.

November 13

What are you believing God to do in your life? Save unsaved loved ones, family or friends, heal your body, deliver you from debt, bless you with a job, car, spouse, house, children…? Now what doubts or fears stand in your way; that God has forgotten what He promised you; God is not concerned with what concerns you; you aren't good enough, saved enough, or worthy to receive from God (who is)? Don't let doubt and fear hinder your faith walk with God. Those who doubt will not receive anything from God.

November 14

God is the awesome creator of the Universe and everything in it. Mankind is created in God's image and each person is a unique creation unto God. No two people are alike. Even identical twins have differences. God made us each special for His purpose and we must give God thanks for our individuality. There is no one else just like you anywhere in the world, there never has been and there never will be. You are a one of a kind master piece. Thank and praise God for all the wonderful gifts and talents He gave you specially!

November 15

When times are rough and hard, praise God. When times are good and easy, praise God. When you are unsure of what to do or how to do it, praise God. When you know exactly what to do and how to do it, praise God. "Let the praises of God continually be in your mouth." The praises that are due God, are not dependent upon how you feel, or what you may or may not be going through. God is due praise because HE is worthy! God is a push over for praise. "Let everything that has breath praise the Lord."

November 16

Many of us miss the call of God on our lives for years and years. We are so busy wanting to be used by God in ministry at church, on our job, in mission fields, hospitals and orphanages that we fail to answer the call for ministering at home. Are you the type of mother, daughter, sister, wife, aunt, cousin, brother, uncle, husband, son or friend that honors and glorifies God in these relationships? Do you treat those closest to you with the same love, kindness, patience and other fruits of the spirit that you do strangers whom you minister or witness to?

November 17

The blood of Jesus will never lose its power. There is no bond like a blood bond. When the enemy attacks, just tell him, "Satan, the blood of Jesus is against you." The blood Jesus shed on Calvary represents a love story of reconciliation. It demonstrates the depth of love God had for His family that was lost, but now is able to come back home because of the Cross of Jesus. "Oh what love, He has for me, that He would give His life." The heavenly Father is patiently waiting for each of us to come back home to Him.

November 18

"You have not because you ask not." What is it that you have not asked God to do in you or for you? As we are on our spiritual journey, we must keep in mind that God's word repeatedly says we are to ask, in faith, and according to His will (the word of God). Because of Jesus, we can boldly go to the throne of grace (with reverence) and make our request made known to God. God delights to give us the desires of our heart, but we must ask in faith and live in holiness.

November 19

Have you told God today how much you love Him? How thankful you are that He chose you before the foundation of the world? How great He is or how awesome His ways are? Does God know that you love Him? Tell God that you love Him and then find someone else and tell them how much God loves them. This will give that person the opportunity to fall in love with God just like you did. Falling in love with Jesus is the best thing anyone could ever do.

November 20

There are two types of bondage, captivity or imprisonment; Physical & Mental. Physical refers to chains, jail or confinement of the body and mental refers to chains, or confinement of the mind. Jesus came to set the captive free, spiritually, physically, and mentally. The Bible tells us that as a person thinks, so is he, or you are what you think. Many people think physical confinement is the worst of the two, but not so. If a person is spiritually and mentally free, then a physical confinement cannot hold them.

November 21

There are many people who are walking around physically free, but have mental and spiritual chains on their minds and souls. This bondage prohibits them from experiencing a sound mind, expressing themselves and freely serving God. To have the mind of Christ is a liberating and exhilarating experience. When problems and issues arise that are out of your control, you don't let them bring you into the bondage of depression, anxiety, or anger. Give it all over to God to work out so that you can be mentally and spiritually free from bondage.

November 22

There is no other way to God except through Jesus Christ. There is no forgiveness for our sins except through Jesus. There is no reconciliation back to God except through Jesus. Jesus is the way, the truth and the life. If Jesus hadn't died on the cross there would be no propitiation for sins, just rituals using dead animals that never satisfied or paid the sin bill. Without Jesus' death, burial, and resurrection, we could never experience or know the depths of God's love or the joy of living in eternity with Him.

November 23

Nature, as a part of the circle of life, consists of four different seasons. Each season is unique in and of itself and plays a vital role in the life of every living thing created by God. Winter is a time of barrenness and hibernation. Spring is a time of rebirth and new beginnings. Summer is a time of abundance and vibrancy. While Fall is a time of planting and storing up things. These four seasons can also be paralleled to the Christian journey. Each of us will experience the different seasons at some point during our Christian walk with God.

November 24

Christians go through seasons of death, loneliness or affliction (winter). We experience seasons of spiritual and physical growth and enlightenment (Spring). We have seasons of abundance, overflow, miracles, excess (summer), and seasons of preparation, gathering, building and encouragement (fall) to help prepare us for a whole new cycle of Seasons. As we grow and mature with the passing of each season, we look back over our lives and discover Gods awesome deliverance and sustaining power.

November 25

Many people, even some Christians, say they don't know how to pray. Praying to God isn't difficult, but it does require a heart and mind to get closer to God. If you are able to form thoughts in your mind (I would like to have a new ______, I hope today my ______ has a great day, I wonder how _______ is doing…), then you can pray. Prayer is taking the self talk you do in your head and reverently (respectfully) saying it or addressing it to God. God is ready and willing to listen and then respond to your prayers.

November 26

As a prayer, the previous thoughts would sound like this: Dear awesome and wonderful God, thank You for being here with me in my heart and mind, I pray that You would forgive me of my sins. Lord I ask for favor and if it is Your will, may I have the new ______. I also pray for Your protection over my loved ones, family and friends. Lord God, deliver and set free______ from ______ and I thank You for Your many wonderful blessings, in Jesus' name, I pray, Amen.

November 27

Do you know the difference between a God experience and a religious experience? A God experience brings about a total life change, both on earth and in the afterlife. But a religious experience may never change thoughts, actions, behaviors or beliefs. A God experience will cause your faith to grow, have a deeper love walk with God and man and will humble your heart. But a religious experience will allow fear to still run your life, selfishness to exist in your heart and pride to guide. Now is your Christian journey a God experience or a religious one?

November 28

How do I praise the Lord? What do I say? You praise God by first acknowledging who He is (the awesome Creator of the universe, mankind, plants, and animals.) Next, you stop to realize how good God has been to you and your loved ones. Then you say "Thank You Lord, You are a good God; awesome are all Your works and I love You. Thank You for blessing me and my family. When I think about Your awesome acts my soul cries Hallelujah." When others see you praising God, they will want to join in; it will be like fire spreading everywhere.

November 29

If you have God called and ordained, Bible based teaching, Holy Ghost filled and led anointed spiritual leaders over your congregation, then you are blessed. You need to stop right now, thank and praise the Lord for having them. Just like having great natural parents is a gift and blessing from God, the same is true of having great spiritual leaders. Great spiritual leaders put God first (not self, position, title, possessions, or money), and they truly care about souls. They desire to see all souls saved, delivered, healed and set free from the bondage of sin.

November 30

Great spiritual leaders spend time fasting, praying and interceding for souls, preaching and teaching the unadulterated Word of God, repenting, and being restored daily in a right relationship with God. They teach their members to have a personal and intimate relationship with God and model this format as well. As Christians, we are always to pray for our leaders and their families. If your leaders are being attacked by the devil and causing Gods Word to be compromised, pray and intercede for their souls as they have done for yours.

December 1

Know matter how much a person prays, fasts, goes to church, reads and studies the bible, does charitable deeds and gives donations; they will NEVER earn salvation. It is a free gift of God. This is the one concept that most people find difficult to accept about Christianity (even some Christians). They feel they must contribute some type of good work or deed to obtain God's gracious gift. But this concept separates God from false religions and makes Him most worthy of our praise. Accept the gift, and thank the Giver.

December 2

Did you know that nothing you have ever done or could ever do is unforgivable with a repentive (sorrowful) heart and mind, under the blood of Jesus? Did you know that you can never get yourself together enough to come to God so that He can accept you? That mindset is a trick of the devil. God called you into His family and predestined your future in Him before the foundations of the world. So pack up your issues, take them on to church, give them to God, then ask Him to deliver and set you free. Then walk in your new freedom.

December 3

Salvation is a free gift of God, but it does cost. It costs our will for God's will. It costs our total submission and obedience to God and His Word. It costs us denying our fleshy desires for God's perfect will. Salvation requires us to be Holy as God is Holy. It requires total trust and dependence on God when we don't know when or where He will move on our behalf. Salvation will cost us giving up and forsaking this sinful world and its ways for a higher calling of God by Christ Jesus. That call is to spread the Good News of Jesus Christ everywhere.

December 4

"Fight the good fight of faith". This scripture lets us know it is a struggle and fight for our faith to daily persevere through doubts, fears, and trials. "But without faith it is impossible to please God." This verse lets us know we can't please God if we don't have faith. "God has given everyone a measure of faith." This verse lets us know every person on earth has some level of faith, even if they choose not to place it in God. "By faith Abraham received the promises of God." This is how we get the promises of God to manifest in our lives.

December 5

There is a war going on! Not the ones fought in the natural world, but the one going on in your mind and body. Your spirit and soul want to serve and obey God. Your body wants to gratify itself perpetually, which most of the time is contrary to the Word of God. This is the war. What God wants from your life and what you want to do with your life rarely agree. So we must kill the fleshly desires or starve them to death, (don't feed into them) nor surrender to them. Instead, feed the spirit with the Word of God, prayer and fasting.

December 6

As believers of God, we should not doubt His promises; continue on in a depressed, lonely, or forsaken state. These are snares the enemy uses to get our minds off of the wonderful blessings God has bestowed upon us. Make a list of all the worries or concerns the enemy brings to your remembrance. Next make a list of all the provisions, blessings, healings, deliverance, and miracles God has done for you within the last month. Now take a look for yourself and see how much bigger and better your God list is. Be sure to include (sight, hearing, touching, smelling…)

December 7

It's not how you start, its how you finish. The race isn't given to the swift, nor the strong, but to those who endure until the very end, shall be saved. Everyone starts their Christian journey at different points. When we were born, some of us were born to wealth, some to poverty, some to loving parents, some to abusive parents, some in health, and some in sickness. But none of us are born free from sin. Everyone will at some point have the opportunity to accept Jesus as Lord and Savior. Whether or not they do determines how they will finish.

December 8

Praise Break:

God I love You and thank You. I glorify Your name with praises of Hallelujah. When I meditate on Your awesome works and glorious power, my eyes fill up with tears of joy and gratitude. Thank You for setting Your compassion and love upon me. I worship and adore You, not because I have already obtained, but because You are faithful, merciful and ever patient. God You have always made a way for me, even when I couldn't see my way through and You will continue to make a way all the days of my life.

December 9

God always answers His children's prayers. But sometimes we may not understand the answer. When we pray and ask God for something and He says yes and grants it, we understand and we are happy. When we pray and ask God for something and He says NO or WAIT, we tend to start rebuking the devil. We have to realize that no and wait ARE answers to our prayers, just not the answers we wanted. We cannot behave like spoiled brats throwing a temper tantrum when our Father tells us no or not right now.

December 10

Obedience is a sacrifice! Our fleshly nature is always in opposition with our spirit nature. God is a spirit and those who worship Him must do so in the spirit as well. The flesh cannot please God, because it always wants to please itself. We must bring our flesh under the obedience of God. This is the sacrifice. Daily we must present our bodies a living sacrifice. Living sacrifices tend to jump off the alter, out of the fire or hot water. We have to determine to stay on the altar to be sacrificed for God's use.

December 11

Waiting on the Lord to fulfill promises, heal, deliver, make a way, etc, requires a willing and patient attitude. But usually God is the One waiting on us to repent, ask, seek, knock, give, etc. If you are waiting on a mate from God, is God waiting on you to start living in holiness? If you are waiting on a financial blessing from God, is God waiting for you to start tithing and sowing seeds? If you are waiting on a healing from God, is God waiting for you to start living a healthier lifestyle? Now who is really waiting on whom?

December 12

How we wait on God to fulfill His promises to us is sometimes key to how long we wait. When we wait on God, but murmur and complain the entire time, then just get comfortable in the wait because God knows we are not ready yet. We have to learn to praise God before the manifestation of the promise appears. God is our Father and He only wants the best for His children, especially growth and maturity. Our attitude toward the timing of God can determine our altitude in God.

December 13

Prayer Break:

Lord God, please forgive me for not doing exactly what You told me to do, when You told me to do it, the exact way You told me to do it! Lord forgive me for putting myself in the place of God and deciding that I knew more or better than You. Forgive me God if I have dropped any souls that You have brought across my path. I pray to be ready to completely obey the next time You decide to use me for the kingdom of Heaven! In Jesus' name I pray, Amen.

December 14

Be careful that you judge not, unless you be judged. In this fallen, sinful world, Christians can sometimes wonder if God really sees and cares about how much evil is going on, and how most people have no problem with it. They call evil good and good evil. But God does see and He does care. God loves us so much that He is allowing sinners to become abased, repent, and turn to Him so He can save their souls in these last days. So don't judge the world and their wickedness, witness to them instead with the love of God. After all, that's what someone did for you!

December 15

God knows our hearts, even when we don't. He loves sinners, but hates sin. God is long suffering (patient) toward us, not wanting any of us to perish (in hell), but rather that we all come to repentance. God sent His only begotten Son into the world, not to condemn it, but to save the world. Christ shed His blood on the Cross for all people, not certain people. If you have never accepted Jesus Christ as Lord and Savior, then you can do so now. Please ask Him to come into your heart and save you from your sins. Giving your life to Him is just that simple.

December 16

The deceptive spirit of busyness runs rampant in the Christian's life today. People are so busy doing so many different things, all day long that they barely have time for themselves, their families or God. The spirit of busyness is a deceptive trick of the enemy to destroy and breakdown family units, intimate relationships with God and the individuals mind, body and spirit. Most of the time they don't see how bad the situation is until trials or death stops them in their tracks. Stop and prioritize your life with God being first, then you, family, work and friends.

December 17

Today's idolatry comes in the form of gluttony, material possessions, work, fame, children, power, money, lust, self, etc. Just because it isn't carved out of wood or stone and we don't carry it with us everywhere we go, talking to it or rubbing it, doesn't make it any less of an idol. Anything or person that we put before God, place a higher value on above God or keeps us from obeying and fully serving God is an idol! God means it when He tells us that we should have no other Gods, but Him. What idols in your life need to be destroyed?

December 18

Did you know that we can also be caught up in religious busyness, just like we can be caught up in worldly busyness? Religious busyness can cause Christians to lose focus of their relationship with God while attending and serving at a local place of worship. We can get so distracted by serving on different church auxiliaries, boards, missions, music ministries, clubs, classes, and organizations that we stop serving and seeking the face of God. We start to serve for and seek after recognition, and acknowledgement of people not God.

December 19

We all want the blessings of God, but we never want to endure the discipline of God. Everywhere you go, you can hear people seeking the blessings of God; "God bless America, or God bless you after a sneeze." But when God disciplines us, most of us act like a three year old who was just denied a treat or toy form the store. We kick and scream, murmur and complain, find fault and judge. We do everything except submit, obey, and humble ourselves under the mighty hand of God, so that He can shape and mold us into vessels of honor.

December 20

Sadly, the moral code of today's society is "if it feels good do it, as long as you aren't hurting anybody." Even worse is, some Christians believe "it doesn't take all that holiness and purity stuff to be a saved Christian and still see God in the afterlife." WRONG! It does take all that and more. We can never let our bodies and emotions dictate how we should live and what we should do; that leads to pure chaos. God made us and He knows that it takes the Holy Spirit to lead us and guide us. We must remember that nothing good dwells in the flesh.

December 21

People sometimes get so caught up in making a name for themselves, obtaining material things, having power and authority, getting married, thin, etc. that they forget that only what is done for God will last. There has yet to be a hearse followed by a U-Haul truck headed to a grave site. You can't take anything with you when you leave. Soon people will forget your name and what you accomplished. Labor to obtain an incorruptible crown that won't perish and set your treasures on high where bugs and worms won't decay it.

December 22

Whatever addiction you face (lust, drugs, food, gambling, alcohol, work, etc.) only a personal relationship with God can satisfy it. Whatever sickness or disease you face, only God can deliver you from it (either through healing or calling you home to be with Him). Whatever trials you face, only God can sustain you. God keeps them in perfect peace whose mind is stayed on Him. There is nothing too hard for God. If you are a born again child of God then you can do all things through Christ who strengthens you.

December 23

I used to believe that bad kids, who grew up to be bad adults came from bad parenting or bad environments. On the flipside, I believed that good kids, who grew up to be good adults came from bible based, involved parents and environments. But Adam and Eve's parent and environment was perfect. This shattered my entire philosophy. God was and is the best parent ever and He only had one Son who obeyed Him without failing, Jesus. Disobedience is a free will choice not always a reflection of parenting skills or environments.

December 24

As Christians we are very blessed and sometimes spoiled. God is so good to us, that even in our trials He always meets our needs. Even if we have lost our jobs, homes, health, or loved one, He still provides for us financially, provides shelter, allows us medical attention or divine healing, sends the Holy Spirit to comfort us and is a Friend that sticks closer than a brother. During a trial, our accommodations may not be what they used to be or what we wished they could be, but we are never destitute or distraught.

December 25

Go tell it on the mountain that Jesus Christ is born. Some critics of the Bible argue that Christ Jesus was not born on this particular day of the calendar year and that celebrating His birth today is inaccurate. So What! He was born, He died, and three days later He rose again! It doesn't matter when the exact date may be on the calendar. We celebrate the miraculous birth not the date on the calendar. Rarely does someone's birthday continuously fall on the weekend, but that is usually the time when they celebrate the fact that they were born, not the date.

December 26

As a Christian, do you realize that you may be the only view of Christ an unbeliever sees? Do you realize you may be the only bible reference they come in contact with? You may be the only expression of God's love that they have ever experienced. You may be the only friend that mirrors the friendship God portrays. You could be the only person an unbeliever knows who lives in the peace of God. Your faith in God may attract the attention of an unbelieving family member or co-worker. Is the light of Jesus shining bright enough to lead someone out of darkness?

December 27

Everything you have or will ever have is all based upon the choices you make. Life is a series of choices. Salvation is a choice, living holy is a choice, and obedience is a choice... God sets before us life and death and we must choose which course we will take. Each of us must choose for ourselves, no one else can make that decision for us. Adam and Eve had a choice, unfortunately they chose death. Jesus also had a choice and fortunately He chose to die to bring us to life. What have you chosen? Tomorrow isn't promised, choose Christ today.

December 28

God doesn't change, His word is still true and He is forever holy. God will not come down to our standards in order to have a relationship with us, we must come up to His. God still calls sin wrong and requires us to repent and turn from sin with a humble heart and remorseful spirit. With God there is no such thing as a little sin. It's either sin or righteousness, no middle ground. God doesn't grade on a curve, He grades on the Cross of Jesus. God desires a lifestyle of holiness, because without it, no one will see God.

December 29

A popular T.V. minister once said "sin will take you further than you want to go, charge you more than you want to pay and keep you longer than you want to stay!" Each of us at some point in our lives have been able to relate to that quote. When the devil presents an opportunity for us to sin against the Word and will of God, he only shows the "cliff notes" version. However, once you accept the sin invitation you realize that the book has way more gory details than you want as a part of your story.

December 30

God doesn't see us the way we see ourselves or as others may see us. God sees us as we relate to Him and His Word (the good, the bad, and the ugly). When we study the Word of God, pray, and seek His face, He transforms and renews our mind to His. Once we begin to have the mind of Christ, we start to see how our lives line up with the Word of God. This is an ongoing process by which God reveals our current state against the characteristics of His Word. Little by little He transforms our image to His.

December 31 *Reflection Notes*

As things draw to a close, stop and pay attention to your structure. Take heed how you build. Christ, the solid rock, is the foundation needed to build your life upon. Without Christ, the foundation will collapse and the structure will be destroyed. Build your life upon the Word of God. Be sure from time to time to monitor your family, fellow church members, friends and neighbors structure to ensure that Christ is also their foundation. We are our brothers and sisters keepers in Christ. Stay saved, safe and submitted in God.

Reflection Notes

Reflection Notes

Reflection Notes

Reflection Notes

LaVergne, TN USA
02 June 2010
184798LV00003B/1/P

9 781427 619037